SHAREPOINT ONLINE ESSENTIALS

PETER AND KATE KALMSTRÖM

Copyright © 2021 Peter Kalmström
ISBN: 9781795314619
All rights reserved

SHAREPOINT ONLINE ESSENTIALS

Welcome to *SharePoint Online Essentials*! This book is intended for SharePoint users who have no administrative roles but need to understand the basics about SharePoint Online. The book explains how to use the common SharePoint Online tools and features, like how to create and manage apps, pages and sites.

SharePoint Online Essentials only covers SharePoint Online basics. The book focuses on the modern SharePoint experience, and the classic experience is only mentioned briefly.

For deeper knowledge about SharePoint, including both experiences, administrator settings and security, I recommend my book *SharePoint Online from Scratch*.

When you study *SharePoint Online Essentials*, I recommend that you, if possible, read the book when you are logged into your SharePoint Online account and can try the features I describe. That will make the learning easier and more varied, and you can directly transfer the book information into usage of your own organization's system.

SharePoint Online is by default a very allowing service, but administrators can restrict the access to certain features. In this book, I have taken the default settings as my starting point.

SharePoint Online is meant to be customized for each organization, so what you see in your system might be different from what I describe here. I hope you still can find your way around, because the basic functionality is the same.

To save space, the images in this book have sometimes been cut where SharePoint only shows blank areas.

I am a developer and systems designer in the first place, not a teacher or author. Therefore, my mother Kate has helped me get the content of *SharePoint Online Essentials* together, so that it is introduced to you in a way that we hope is easy to read and understand.

Kate is a former teacher and author of textbooks, so she knows how to explain things in a pedagogic way. She has worked with SharePoint Online in our family business for many years and have seen the product develop.

I have had the last word and approved of all the final text in this book, and it is my "voice" you hear. And of course, I take the full responsibility for the technical content and for the correctness of everything said about SharePoint Online in *SharePoint Online Essentials*.

Good luck with your studies!

Peter Kalmström

TABLE OF CONTENTS

1 INTRODUCTION 10
   1.1 ADD CONTENT 10
2 THE 365 NAVIGATION BAR 11
   2.1 THE LEFT NAVIGATION BAR 11
      2.1.1 The App Launcher *11*
      2.1.2 The SharePoint Online Start Page *12*
         2.1.2.1 Follow Sites 13
         2.1.2.2 Save for Later 13
   2.2 THE SEARCH BOX 14
      2.2.1 Search from an App *14*
   2.3 THE RIGHT NAVIGATION BAR 15
      2.3.1 Settings Icon *15*
      2.3.2 Question Mark *15*
      2.3.3 Profile Picture *16*
   2.4 SUMMARY 17
3 SHAREPOINT APPS 18
   3.1 SELECT AN ITEM 19
   3.2 VIEW MODES 19
      3.2.1 Standard View Mode *20*
         3.2.1.1 Information Pane 20
      3.2.2 Grid View Mode *21*
   3.3 MODERN AND CLASSIC APP INTERFACE 21
      3.3.1 Differences *22*
   3.4 ADD AN APP 22
   3.5 APP SETTINGS 24
      3.5.1 App Link in the Site navigation *25*
   3.6 COLUMNS 26
      3.6.1 Create a Column *26*
         3.6.1.1 Create Column from the App Settings 26
         3.6.1.2 Create Column from the Grid View Mode 28
         3.6.1.3 Create Column from the Standard View Mode 28
      3.6.2 Character Limits in Text Columns *29*
      3.6.3 Column Types *30*
         3.6.3.1 Date and Time Column 30
         3.6.3.2 Choice Column 31
         3.6.3.3 Location Column 32
      3.6.4 Edit a Column *33*
      3.6.5 Edit Column Values *34*

	3.6.5.1	Edit Multiple Items	34
3.6.6		Filter, Sort and Group	35
3.6.7		Format a Column	36
	3.6.7.1	Data Bars	38
	3.6.7.2	Conditional Formatting	38
3.6.8		Rename a Column	38
3.6.9		Edit the Form	39
3.7	VIEWS		40
3.7.1		The View Selector	41
	3.7.1.1	Create a New View	42
3.7.2		Edit a View	44
	3.7.2.1	Totals	46
3.8	ALERTS		48
3.9	DELETE AND RESTORE APP CONTENT		49
3.9.1		Delete an Item	49
3.9.2		Delete a Column	49
3.9.3		Delete a View	50
3.9.4		Delete an App	50
3.9.5		Restore Deleted Content	50
	3.9.5.1	Second-Stage Bin	51
3.10	VERSION HISTORY		51
3.10.1		See Version History	52
3.10.2		Version History in Library Apps	53
3.10.3		Version History in List Apps	54
3.11	SUMMARY		54

4 LIST APPS 55

4.1	COMMAND BAR BUTTONS		55
4.1.1		No Item Selected	55
	4.1.1.1	Export to Excel	56
4.1.2		One Item Selected	56
	4.1.2.1	Edit	56
	4.1.2.2	Comment	57
	4.1.2.3	Copy Link	58
4.1.3		Multiple Items Selected	58
4.2	CREATE A NEW LIST ITEM		58
4.3	MICROSOFT LISTS		59
4.3.1		Create a New List App	60
	4.3.1.1	Blank List	61
	4.3.1.2	From Excel	62
	4.3.1.3	From Existing List	62
	4.3.1.4	From Template	63
4.4	THE MULTI-LINE COLUMN		64
4.4.1		Rich Text	64
4.4.2		Append Changes to Existing Text	65

		4.4.2.1	Enable Append 66
4.5	The Tasks List 66
	4.5.1	Tasks and Issue Tracking Alerts 67
4.6	The Calendar List 68
	4.6.1	Calendar Views 68
	4.6.2	Create a New Event 69
	4.6.3	Edit an Event 69
4.7	Summary 69

5 LIBRARY APPS 70

5.1	Why Document Libraries? 71
5.2	Library Unique Features 71
	5.2.1 No Item Selected 72
	5.2.2 One Item Selected 72
	5.2.3 Document Tile 73
5.3	Create a Library App 74
	5.3.1 Auto-Created Columns 74
	5.3.1.1 The Title Column and the Search Engine 75
5.4	Add Content to Document Libraries 75
	5.4.1 Upload Files 76
	5.4.1.1 Select Multiple Files 76
	5.4.1.2 Upload Button 76
	5.4.1.3 Drag and Drop 76
	5.4.1.4 Save a File to SharePoint 77
	5.4.2 Rename a File 78
	5.4.3 Create an Office File in a Library 79
	5.4.3.1 Naming 80
5.5	Find a File Link 81
5.6	Edit a File or an Item 81
	5.6.1 Edit Properties 81
	5.6.2 Edit an Office File 81
	5.6.2.1 Editing by Multiple Users 82
5.7	Check Out / Check In 82
	5.7.1 Check Out / Check In Commands 83
	5.7.2 Require Check Out 83
5.8	Copy Items 84
5.9	'+New' Menu Options 84
	5.9.1 Upload Office Template 84
	5.9.2 Edit the '+New' Menu 85
5.10	Summary 85

6 SHAREPOINT SITES 86

6.1	Site Terms 86
	6.1.1 Homepage 86
	6.1.2 Home Site 86

		6.1.3 Site and Site Collection *87*
6.2	SITE TYPES 87
	6.2.1	*Group Team Site* *87*
		6.2.1.1 Microsoft 365 Group 88
		6.2.1.2 Microsoft Teams 89
	6.2.2	*Communication Site* *89*
		6.2.2.1 Templates 89
6.3	CREATE A SITE 90
	6.3.1	*Team Site* *91*
	6.3.2	*Communication site* *92*
6.4	SITE CONTENTS 93
6.5	SITE SETTINGS 94
6.6	CHANGE THE LOOK¨ 95
6.7	HUB FAMILIES 96
	6.7.1	*Associate with a Hub Site* *97*
	6.7.2	*Hub Permissions* *97*
6.8	SUBSITES 98
6.9	NAVIGATION 98
	6.9.1	*Edit the Navigation* *98*
	6.9.2	*Site Navigation Hierarchy* *101*
6.10	DELETE AND RESTORE A SITE 101
6.11	SUMMARY 102

7   ONEDRIVE FOR BUSINESS 103

7.1	THE "MY FILES" LIBRARY 103
7.2	USER SETTINGS 104
	7.2.1 *Restore OneDrive* *105*
7.3	SHARING FROM ONEDRIVE 107
7.4	SYNCHRONIZE WITH A LOCAL FOLDER 108
	7.4.1 *First Sync between a SharePoint Library and a Folder* *108*
	7.4.2 *Sync Issues* *111*
	7.4.3 *Sync Settings* *111*
	7.4.3.1 Files On-Demand 111
7.5	CREATE A SITE 113
7.6	MULTIPLE LIBRARIES BENEFITS 115
7.7	SUMMARY 115

8   SITE PAGES 116

8.1	THE "SITE PAGES" LIBRARY 116
	8.1.1 *Check Out* *117*
	8.1.2 *Version History* *118*
	8.1.3 *Scheduled Page Publishing* *118*
	8.1.4 *Copy a Page* *119*
	8.1.5 *Set a Page as Homepage* *120*

- 8.2 CREATE A PAGE 120
  - 8.2.1 Page Templates 121
    - 8.2.1.1 Save a Page as a Template 122
  - 8.2.2 Edit Mode 123
  - 8.2.3 Title Area 124
  - 8.2.4 Comments 124
  - 8.2.5 Sections 125
  - 8.2.6 Edit Sections and Web Parts 126
  - 8.2.7 Add Web Parts 126
  - 8.2.8 Add Content to Web Parts 127
    - 8.2.8.1 Add Image or File 128
  - 8.2.9 Web Part Examples 129
    - 8.2.9.1 365 Apps 129
    - 8.2.9.2 Button and Call to action 129
    - 8.2.9.3 Divider 129
    - 8.2.9.4 Document Library and List 129
    - 8.2.9.5 Hero 130
    - 8.2.9.6 Highlighted Content 132
    - 8.2.9.7 Spacer 132
  - 8.2.10 Page Details 133
  - 8.2.11 Promote a Page 134
  - 8.2.12 The News Web Part 135
    - 8.2.12.1 Create a News Post 135
    - 8.2.12.2 Create a News Link 136
  - 8.2.13 Spaces 136
- 8.3 ADD LINKS TO A PAGE 137
  - 8.3.1 The Link Web Part 137
  - 8.3.2 The Quick Links Web Part 137
  - 8.3.3 The Highlighted Content Web Part 138
  - 8.3.4 The Sites Web Part 138
- 8.4 ADD IMAGES TO PAGES 139
  - 8.4.1 Picture Options for Pages 139
    - 8.4.1.1 Image Web Part 139
    - 8.4.1.2 Image Gallery Web Part 140
    - 8.4.1.3 Document Library Web Part 141
- 8.5 SUMMARY 141

9 PERMISSIONS AND SHARING 142

- 9.1 INHERITANCE 142
- 9.2 SHAREPOINT GROUPS 142
- 9.3 SHARE A SITE 144
  - 9.3.1 Default Site Permissions 144
  - 9.3.2 Share a Site with the Share Button 144
  - 9.3.3 Share a Site from the Site Permissions Pane 145
    - 9.3.3.1 Share from Communication Site 145

  9.3.3.2 Share from Group Team Site 145
 9.3.4 Share a Group Team Site with an External Guest 146
 9.3.5 Manage Site Members 147
  9.3.5.1 Manage Communication Site Members 147
  9.3.5.2 Manage Group Team Site Members 147
 9.3.6 Site Sharing Permissions 148
  9.3.6.1 Access Request 149
9.4 SHARE A FILE 149
 9.4.1 The 'Share' Command 150
 9.4.2 Share with a Link 152
 9.4.3 Manage Access 152
 9.4.4 E-mail Attachments 153
9.5 SHARE A PAGE 154
9.6 STOP SHARING AN ITEM 155
9.7 SUMMARY 156

10 POWER AUTOMATE BUILT-IN FLOWS 157

10.1 REMINDER 157
10.2 REQUEST SIGN-OFF 159
10.3 APPROVE/REJECT PAGES 160
 10.3.1 Configure the Flow 161
 10.3.2 Process 162
 10.3.3 Turn Off Page Approval 163
10.4 SUMMARY 163

11 THE FORMS SURVEY 164

11.1 CREATE A FORM 164
 11.1.1 Edit 165
 11.1.2 Branching 165
11.2 SHARE THE FORM 166
11.3 CHECK FORM RESULTS 167
11.4 FORM SETTINGS 167
11.5 SUMMARY 168

ABOUT THE AUTHORS 169

INDEX 170

1 INTRODUCTION

SharePoint is Microsoft's platform for enterprise content management and sharing. SharePoint is also a place for social networking within organizations.

The cloud edition of SharePoint is called SharePoint Online and is included in most Microsoft 365 and Office 365 subscriptions. When your organization subscribes to Microsoft/Office 365, the organization has a tenant in the cloud, where all the content is stored.

All content in SharePoint is contained in sites. Each site has pages, where you can reach and work with the content.

Home
Conversations
Documents
Notebook
Pages
Site contents
Recycle bin
Edit

You can reach the content in a site that you have access to from links in the Site navigation. This navigation is placed either to the left or on top of each page.

In settings pages, the Site navigation is sometimes called "Quick Launch".

You can also reach all content you have access to from the Site contents of each site. There is often a link to the Site contents in the Site navigation. We will come back to both Site navigation and Site contents in chapter 6, SharePoint Sites.

This book describes how you can manage and create new content in sites and share content with others.

1.1 ADD CONTENT

One of the most important reasons for using SharePoint, is that you want to share data and documents within an organization. Most often, you share content with either a group of people within the tenant or with everyone in the tenant.

These are the most common methods to add content and share it among colleagues within the same tenant:

- Create a new document directly in a SharePoint library app or upload an existing document to a SharePoint library.
- Add info to a SharePoint list app, for example a team tasks list.
- Create a news post for the home page of a SharePoint site.
- Add a comment to a list, an Office file or a page.
- Add or edit SharePoint pages. You can fill your pages with text, images, links or videos.

There will be more information and examples of these ways to share information throughout the book.

2 THE 365 NAVIGATION BAR

When you start reading this book, you have probably received a Microsoft 365 or Office 365 account and have access to your organization's SharePoint Online tenant.

Microsoft/Office 365 includes many more services than SharePoint, and in this section, we will look at the navigation bar that is common for all 365 apps and services. This navigation bar is present on top of each page, almost everywhere in Microsoft/Office 365.

2.1 THE LEFT NAVIGATION BAR

The left 365 navigation bar has two parts: the App launcher or start menu and the name of the current service.

2.1.1 The App Launcher

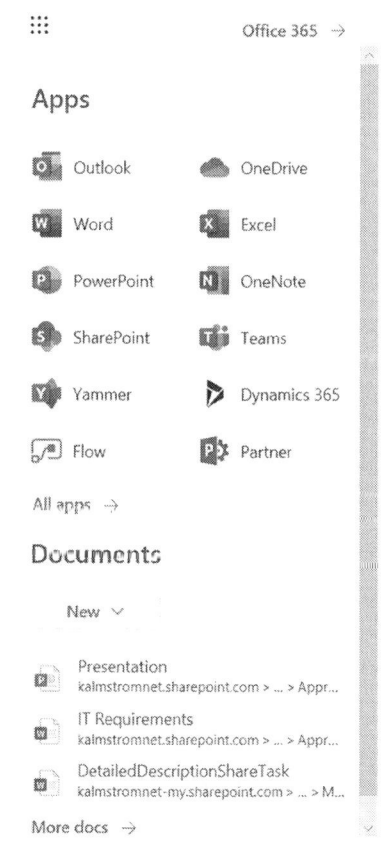

You can reach all 365 services you have access to by clicking on the App launcher in the left corner of the 365 navigation bar.

Services that are relevant to users and much used are shown with icons in the launcher.

Below the icons, there is a link to all apps, a button for document creation and links to your recent documents.

When you click on an icon in the App launcher, the corresponding service will open in the same tab.

11

When you hover the mouse over an icon, three dots, a so called ellipsis, will be visible.

Click on the ellipsis at an icon, if you want to open the service in a new tab in the browser, unpin it from the launcher (so that it is not visible there anymore) or learn more.

Microsoft 365

Outlook — OneDrive

Word — Open in new tab

PowerPoint — Unpin from launcher

SharePoint — Learn more — Teams

2.1.2 The SharePoint Online Start Page

When you click on the SharePoint icon in the 365 App launcher, or on 'SharePoint' in the left part of the 365 navigation bar, you will be directed to the SharePoint Online start page..

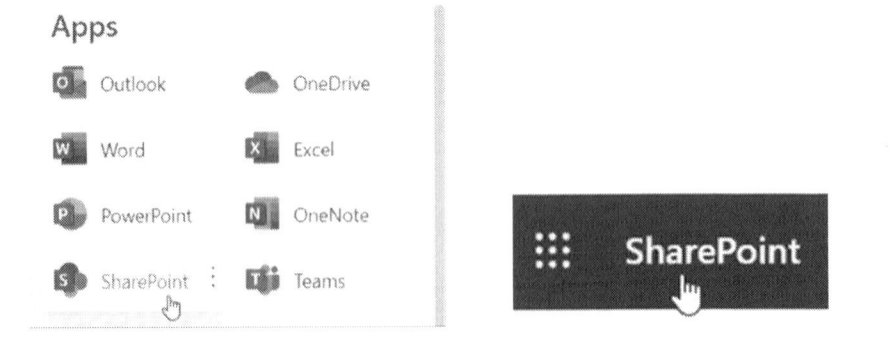

Apps

Outlook   OneDrive
Word   Excel
PowerPoint OneNote
SharePoint Teams

SharePoint

The SharePoint Online start page is a kind of SharePoint Favorites page. Here, you can find links to SharePoint sites that you have created or that you have decided to follow, to your recent or frequently used sites, to news and to sites promoted by the organization.

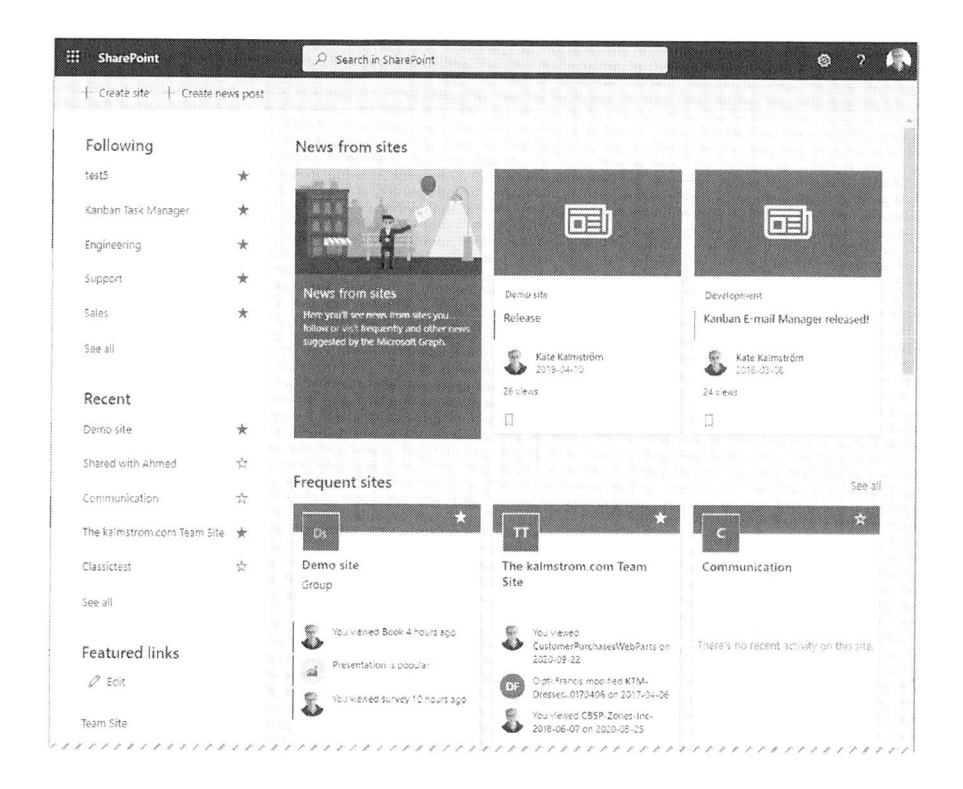

2.1.2.1 Follow Sites

To follow a site from the SharePoint Online start page, click on the star to the right of the site icon. (Click again to stop follow the site.)

To follow an open site, click on 'Not following' in the top right corner of the page.

2.1.2.2 Save for Later

The "Save for later" feature gives you a way to bookmark news and documents that are displayed in the SharePoint Online start page.

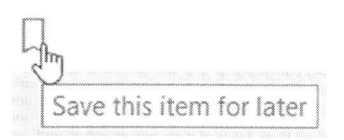

When you click on the icon, the notation will change to "Saved for later", and the item will be visible under its own heading in the left menu of the SharePoint Online start page. If you click on the icon again, the entry will be removed from the left menu.

Saved for later

Latest on the election

2.2 THE SEARCH BOX

There is a search field in the middle of the 365 navigation bar. If you have a small screen, the search field is replaced with a magnifying icon that opens a search field over the whole navigation bar.

The search box suggests results even before you start typing, based on your recent activity, and it updates the suggestions as you type. If you don't select one of the suggestions, the process continues in several steps:

1. There is a suggestion to show more results.

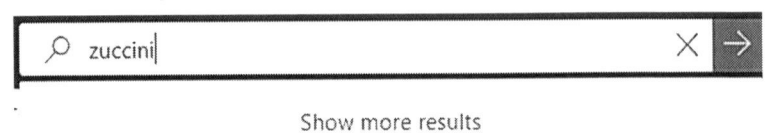

   > zuccini

   Show more results

2. The expanded search takes you to a Search center. It has the verticals All, Files, Sites and News.

   Organization > The kalmstrom.com Team Site

   All   Files   Sites   News   ▽ Filters

3. You get a chance to search the whole tenant.

   We couldn't find any results for zuccini

   Search the whole organization for zuccini

4. Now the Search center also gets verticals for People and Power BI.

The Search center 'All' and 'Files' verticals give the possibility to filter by latest modified time: Any time, Past month, Past 3 months and Past year.

2.2.1 Search from an App

When you start the search from the navigation bar above an app, the app items are searched first. If there are hits in the app, the app content is filtered to show only items that matches the search.

2.3 THE RIGHT NAVIGATION BAR

On the right side of the 365 navigation bar, there are different icons. Wherever you are in Microsoft/Office 365, you will see your own profile picture or an icon with your initials far to the right.

Most often there is also a Settings icon and a question mark. On small screens, the settings and help icons are placed under an ellipsis.

In addition to the 365 icons, SharePoint pages also have a megaphone icon to the left of the settings icon. When you click on it, you will get suggestions on next steps, such as add team members and post news. You can see this icon on the image below.

2.3.1 Settings Icon

The Settings icon on the right side of the 365 navigation bar opens a right pane with different content depending on service.

In SharePoint, the 365 Settings icon shows links to add a new app or page, to see site information and content and more.

There are also personal settings for theme, language, time zone (by default, 365 gets the same regional settings as your computer), password and contact preferences.

If you change your 365 theme, your selected theme will only be shown to you.

2.3.2 Question Mark

Under the question mark icon in the 365 navigation bar, you can find help articles from Microsoft.

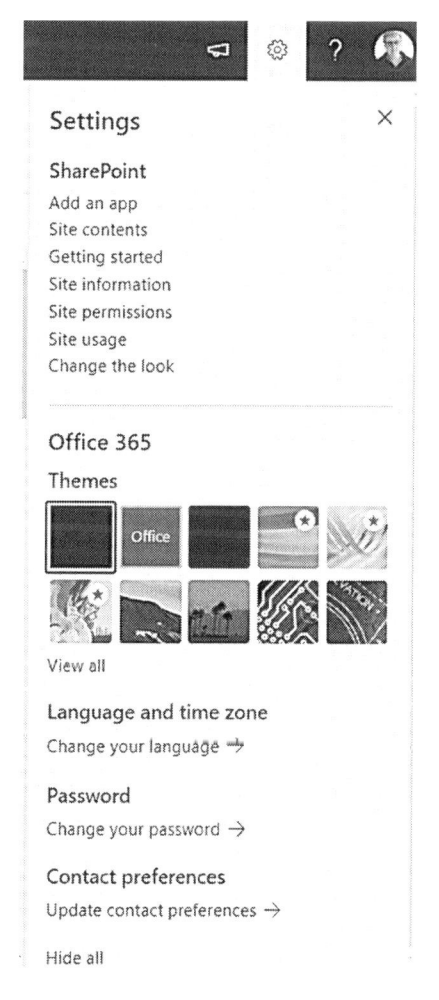

Settings

SharePoint
Add an app
Site contents
Getting started
Site information
Site permissions
Site usage
Change the look

Office 365

Themes

View all

Language and time zone
Change your language →

Password
Change your password →

Contact preferences
Update contact preferences →

Hide all

15

2.3.3   Profile Picture

When you are new to Microsoft/Office 365, the icon far to the right in the navigation bar has you initials. They are meant to be replaced with your photo, as you can see in the images above. The photo (or initials) will be show in various contexts across the tenant.

Click on the icon to have options. In SharePoint, the options under the profile picture are 'View account' and 'My Office profile'.

It is also under your profile picture that you should sign out when you want to leave Microsoft 365.

- Click in the profile picture to add your photo, or to change it.
- Click on 'View account' to find details about your account.
- 'My Office profile', opens the Delve site, where you should add and edit information about yourself that is useful and relevant to your colleagues.

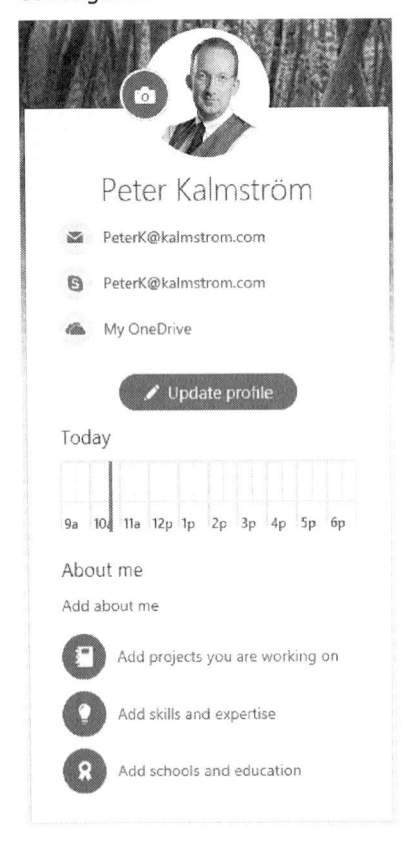

16

The information will be shown in various ways to people that you cooperate within the organization.

Here you can also find links to your recent work and to people in the organization that you have cooperated with.

2.4 SUMMARY

The navigation bar that you can find on top of most Microsoft 365 apps and services is important for making them look like one unit. In this chapter, you have learned how to use the different parts of the 365 navigation bar.

In the continuation of this book, the 365 Settings icon will be the most mentioned part of the navigation bar. When you start use SharePoint Online in your daily work, the Search box and the link to the SharePoint Online start page will probably be more important to you, but you will make use of the links under the 365 Settings icon too.

In the next three chapters, you will learn how to manage SharePoint Online apps, and we will start with a chapter that describes what all apps have in common.

3 SHAREPOINT APPS

SharePoint content can be stored and shared in apps. Document libraries, picture libraries, contact lists and calendars are all examples of apps, and all app types have common features.

A SharePoint app is like a database table or spreadsheet. Data is distributed in rows, and each row is known as an item. The image below shows part of a list app, where you can see four items.

Department Name	Manager	Staff
South	Peter Kalmström	15
North	Peter Kalmström	200
East	Kate Kalmström	50
West	Kate Kalmström	4

Each row, or item, has various columns where you can enter metadata, called values or properties, that describe the item. This information is used by the search crawler to update the search index, so metadata plays an important role to make content easy to find.

The value in one of the columns, usually the first column from the left, becomes underlined when you hover the mouse over it. Click on this value to open the item in a list app or the file in a library app. The image below comes from a library.

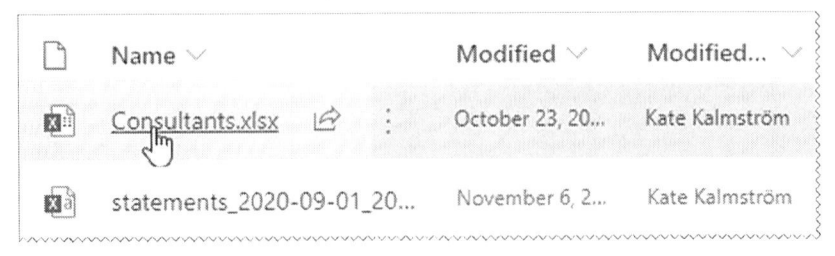

	Name	Modified	Modified...
	Consultants.xlsx	October 23, 20...	Kate Kalmström
	statements_2020-09-01_20...	November 6, 2...	Kate Kalmström

In this chapter, I will explain what is common for both app types:
- The app settings page
- The Standard and Grid view modes
- Columns, filter and sort
- Views
- Alerts
- Version history

In the next two chapters, we will have a closer look at list apps and library apps.

If you create your own app to test the features I describe in this chapter – which is something I strongly recommend! – you should start with creating a custom list app via the 'Add an app' command, as described in section 3.6, Add an App. That app type has all the features described in this chapter but no other features that might disturb your learning process. There will be time to create other apps later in this book.

When you create a new item in an app, the metadata is filled out in a form. This is done a bit differently for list apps and library apps, so I will describe the item creation in the following two chapters.

Apps can be embedded in SharePoint pages, and that is something I will come back to later in the book.

Note that SharePoint apps are normally shared within a group of people – that is the main point of SharePoint, after all! – so use them for information that should be shared, not for personal data. An exception to that, is apps in your personal OneDrive for Business site, which is described in chapter 7.

3.1 SELECT AN ITEM

Sometimes, you must select an item before you can do something with it. You can select items in lists and libraries by clicking in the ring to the left in the item row.

When you select an item, the buttons in the command bar will change. How that is done, is different for list apps and library apps, so we will come back to that in chapter 4 and 5.

In chapter 4 and 5, I will also explain how you can create and edit items in lists and libraries.

focuses on the modern SharePoint experience. The classic experience is only mentioned briefly.

3.2 VIEW MODES

App content can be displayed in Standard or Grid view mode. You can create new items and edit items from both view modes.

3.2.1 Standard View Mode

The Standard view mode is shown by default when you open an app. In the Standard view mode, each item has an ellipsis (…). It is normally placed to the right in the first column from the left.

The ellipsis becomes visible when you hover the mouse cursor over the item.

When you click on the ellipsis, you can see options for what to do with the item and information about it. The options are different, depending on what kind of app it is. The image above comes from a list app.

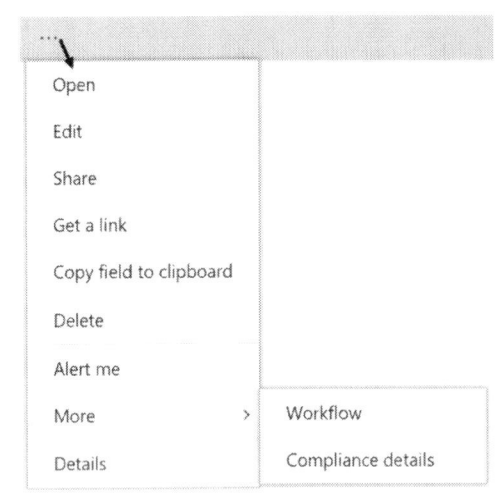

3.2.1.1 Information Pane

In the Standard view mode, each item has an Information pane to the right.

Select an item and click on the information icon in the right part of the command bar to open this pane. You can also select 'Details' under the item ellipsis, see the image above.

In the Information pane, you can see and edit details about the item, such as the item properties and who has access to the item. You can also see recent activity for the item and more.

In library apps, there is a preview of the file in the item on top of the Information pane, like in the image to the right.

When no item has been selected in the app, the Information pane for lists shows who has access to the list. The Information pane for libraries shows the latest activity in the library.

3.2.2 Grid View Mode

Click on the 'Edit in grid view' button in the command bar to reach the Grid view mode.

⊞ Edit in grid view

When an app is show in the Grid view mode, it looks like a spreadsheet, and you can add and edit items directly in the cells.

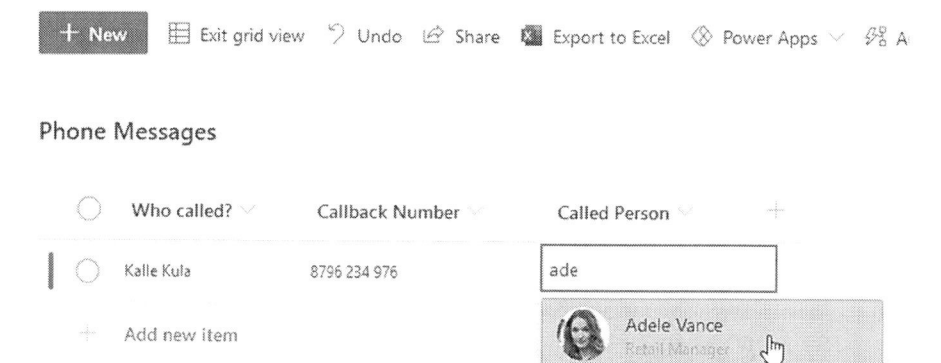

Phone Messages

The Grid view mode is especially powerful if you are used to work with Excel. Copy and paste, as well as some fill commands, work in this view.

The Grid view shows 100 items on each page.
If the app has more items, there is a "next page" arrow below the last item on the page.   ⟨ 401 - 500 ⟩

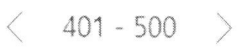

The grid interface has 'Undo' and 'Redo' buttons, so that you can regret and repeat actions. Ctrl + Z and Ctrl + Y (Windows) and Command + Z and Command + Shift + Z (Mac OS) will work as well.

⊞ Exit grid view   ✏ Edit   ↶ Undo

The command bar has an 'Exit grid view' button in the Grid view mode. Click on that button when you are finished with the editing, and the list will go back to the Standard view mode with all your changes saved.

3.3 MODERN AND CLASSIC APP INTERFACE

Almost all apps give a possibility to use either a modern or a classic interface. When that is possible, there is a switch link under the Site navigation.

Modern interface link:

Return to classic SharePoint

Classic interface link:

Exit classic experience

21

In this book, we will focus on the more common modern app interface, but if your organization prefers the classic interface, I am sure you can figure it out. The basic features are the same.

3.3.1 Differences

The most obvious difference between the modern and the classic interface is that the classic interface has a ribbon, with the commands grouped under tabs. The modern app interface, instead have a command bar, also called "quick actions pane".

The command bar in the modern app interface has three features that are not available in the classic ribbon:

⊗ Power Apps ∨   ⁂ Automate ∨   ···   ≡ All Items ∨   ▽   ⓘ

- The 'Power Apps' command lets you create a powerapp from the app and customize the app form in an advanced manner. Power Apps is out of scope for this book.
- The 'Automate' command lets you create a flow connected to the app and reach the flows you own, *refer to* chapter 10.
- The Information pane, where you can see information about the whole app or see and change information about a selected item, as described above.

We will take a closer look at the command bars for list and library apps later in this book.

Another important difference between the two app experiences is that most of the settings and editing in apps with the modern interface is performed in a right pane, like the Information pane.

The right pane opens on various commands, and to close it you can either click on the 'Save' button to save your changes or on the X in the top right corner to close the pane without saving.

The classic interface opens a dialog or a new page in these situations.

3.4 ADD AN APP

Microsoft has made it easy to create new apps in SharePoint Online, because you can use a template and modify it to suit your needs. Each new app will be placed inside the SharePoint site where you created it.

Below, I will describe general app creation. There are also specific creation options for lists and libraries, and I will come back to them in the chapters about specific features for these apps.

1. Open the 365 Settings icon and select 'Add an app'.

You can also click on '+ New' and then 'App' on a homepage or in the Site contents.

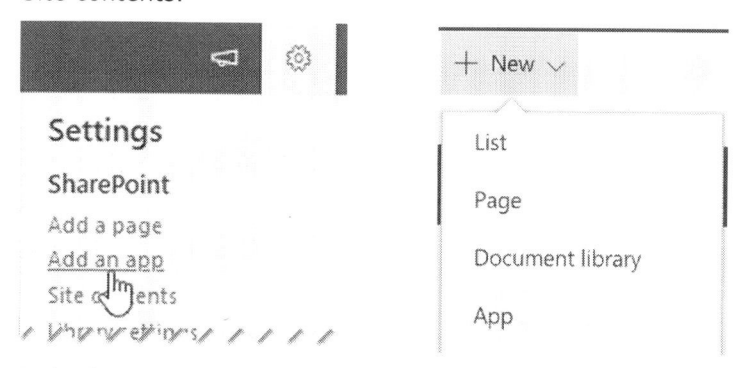

In both cases, you will be directed to the "Your Apps" page.

2. In the "Your Apps" page, search for a template that is similar to the app you want to create. Click on the icon to create the new app. When you select the option 'Custom List', the new app will only have a "Title" column. Other templates will have more columns added from start.

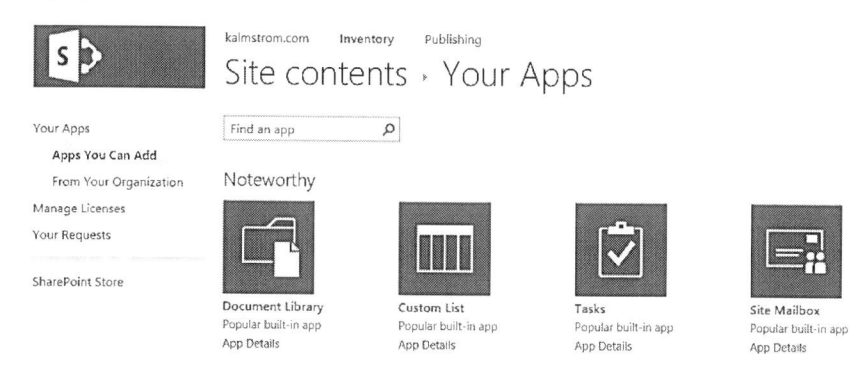

3. Give the app a name and click on 'Create'. If you click on the 'Advanced Options' link, you can give a description of the new app. Some app templates also have a few settings under 'Advanced Options'.

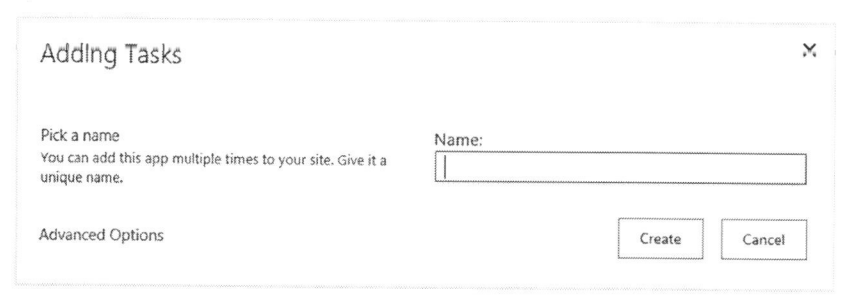

When the new app has been created in this way, it will not be opened automatically. Instead, you will be directed to the Site contents, where you can open the app or its settings.

3.5 APP SETTINGS

Each app has a settings page where you can find many kinds of settings, including settings for columns and views.

You can reach the settings for all app types from the Site contents, where you are directed when you have created a new app from the "Your Apps" page. Click on the ellipsis to the right of the app name or title and select Settings.

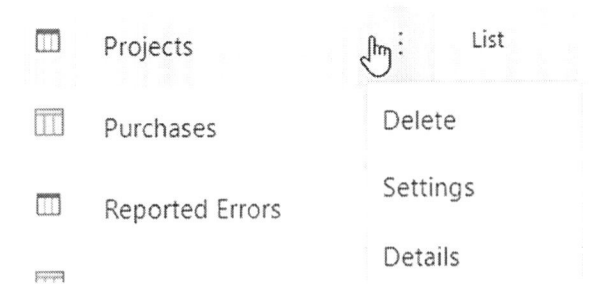

When you have the app open, there is a settings link under the 365 Settings icon. In list apps the link text is 'List settings' and in library apps the text is 'Library settings'.

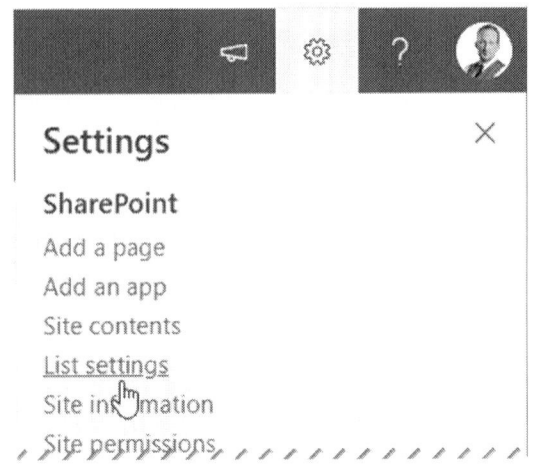

The settings pages are a bit different depending on app type, but all app settings show the app's columns and views and give a possibility to open and customize them.

List Information

Name: Documents
Web Address: https://m365x446726.sharepoint.com/sites/DigitalInitiativePublicRelations/Shared Documents/Forms/AllItems.asp:
Description:

General Settings	Permissions and Management	Communications
▫ List name, description and navigation	▫ Permissions for this document library	▫ RSS settings
▫ Versioning settings	▫ Manage files which have no checked in version	
▫ Advanced settings	▫ Information Rights Management	
▫ Validation settings	▫ Workflow Settings	
▫ Column default value settings	▫ Apply label to items in this list or library	
▫ Audience targeting settings	▫ Enterprise Metadata and Keywords Settings	
▫ Rating settings		
▫ Form settings		

Columns

A column stores information about each document in the document library. The following columns are currently available in this document library:

Column (click to edit)	Type	Required
Title	Single line of text	
Modified	Date and Time	
Created	Date and Time	
Created By	Person or Group	
Modified By	Person or Group	
Checked Out To	Person or Group	

▫ Create column
▫ Add from existing site columns
▫ Column ordering
▫ Indexed columns

Views

A view of a document library allows you to see a particular selection of items or to see the items sorted in a particular order. Views currently configured for this document library:

View (click to edit)	Default View	Mobile View	Default Mobile View
All Documents	✓	✓	✓

▫ Create view

3.5.1 App Link in the Site navigation

It is often suitable to have a link to the app in the site's Site navigation, so that the app is easy to find and reach by everyone who has access to it.

When you create an app from the "Your Apps" page, the new app at first shows up in the Site navigation under 'Recent', but you must add it to the Site navigation in the app settings to make it stay:

1. Open the app settings in one of the two ways described above.
2. Click on the link 'List name, description and navigation' under the General Settings heading.

General Settings

- List name, description and navigation
- Versioning settings

3. In the new page that opens, select the 'Yes' radio button for display in the Site navigation – here called Quick Launch.

Navigation

Specify whether a link to this list appears in the Quick Launch. Note: it only appears if Quick Launch is used for navigation on your site.

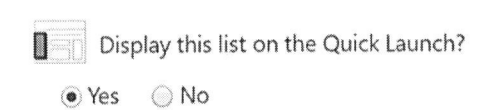

Display this list on the Quick Launch?
● Yes ○ No

4. Click on 'Save'.

3.6 COLUMNS

Information about each app item is kept in columns. The column content is often referred to as values, metadata or properties. The columns are generally the same for all items in the app, but all items might not have a value in each column.

When you add a new item to an app, you fill out the metadata in a form where each column is represented by a field. In this book, I will therefore use the term "column" when talking about the app interface and "field" when I refer to the form where the metadata is filled out.

In library apps, you can create a new item by just adding a file to the library, but you should always edit the new item and fill out any metadata columns.

3.6.1 Create a Column

When you create a column, you must always select a column type. The type depends on what kind of metadata the column should contain, like numbers, dates or hyperlinks.

The default column type is 'Single line of text', but there are many other options. Columns can be created in several different ways.

3.6.1.1 Create Column from the App Settings

All existing columns are displayed in the app settings, and here you can also see of which type each column is. Below the existing columns, there is a link to create a new column.

Column (click to edit)	Type
Title	Single line of text
Modified	Date and Time
Created	Date and Time
Callback Number	Single line of text
Caller Name	Single line of text
Called Person	Person or Group
Returned?	Choice
Created By	Person or Group
Modified By	Person or Group

⬚ Create column ⬅

The 'Create column' link in the app settings, opens a "Create Column" page.

Give the column a name and select column type.

Then you will have different options depending on what type of column you selected.

The image below shows the options for the default column type, Single line of text.

Fill out the fields and select your options.

Then click OK at the bottom of the page to finish creating the new column.

Settings ▸ Create Column ⓘ

Name and Type
Type a name for this column, and select the type of information you want to store in the column.

Column name:
[   ]

The type of information in this column is:
- ● Single line of text
- ○ Multiple lines of text
- ○ Choice (menu to choose from)
- ○ Number (1, 1.0, 100)
- ○ Currency ($, ¥, €)
- ○ Date and Time
- ○ Lookup (information already on this site)
- ○ Yes/No (check box)
- ○ Person or Group
- ○ Hyperlink or Picture
- ○ Calculated (calculation based on other columns)
- ○ Task Outcome
- ○ External Data
- ○ Managed Metadata

Additional Column Settings
Specify detailed options for the type of information you selected.

Description:
[   ]

Require that this column contains information:
○ Yes ● No

Enforce unique values:
○ Yes ● No

Maximum number of characters:
[255]

Default value:
● Text ○ Calculated Value
[   ]

☑ Add to all content types
☑ Add to default view

27

3.6.1.2 Create Column from the Grid View Mode

In the app interface in Grid view mode, click on the plus sign to the right of the existing columns. Now you will have some column type options.

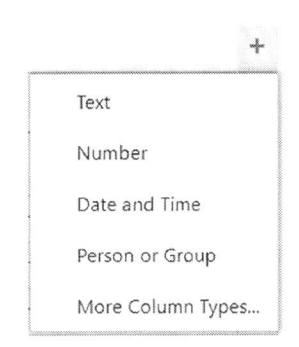

When you click on one of the options, a new cell will be created where you can add the column name.

You can also add values for the existing items in the cells below the column name, but you must go to the Standard view mode and edit the column to make any column settings.

```
Text
Number
Date and Time
Person or Group
More Column Types...
```

'More Column Types…' in the dropdown directs you to the "Create Column" page.

3.6.1.3 Create Column from the Standard View Mode

In Standard view mode, click on '+ Add column'. Now you will have more options than in the Grid view mode.

When you click on one of the visible options, a right pane will open. It has the most common settings, and you can find more when you expand 'More options'.

When you click on 'More…' in the dropdown, you will be directed to in the "Create Column" page.

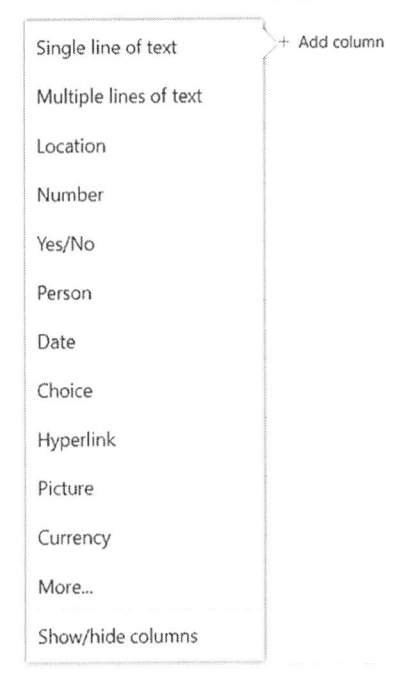

```
Single line of text
Multiple lines of text
Location
Number
Yes/No
Person
Date
Choice
Hyperlink
Picture
Currency
More...
Show/hide columns
```

28

In Standard view mode, you can also open the dropdown at one of the existing columns and select 'Column settings' >'Add a column'.

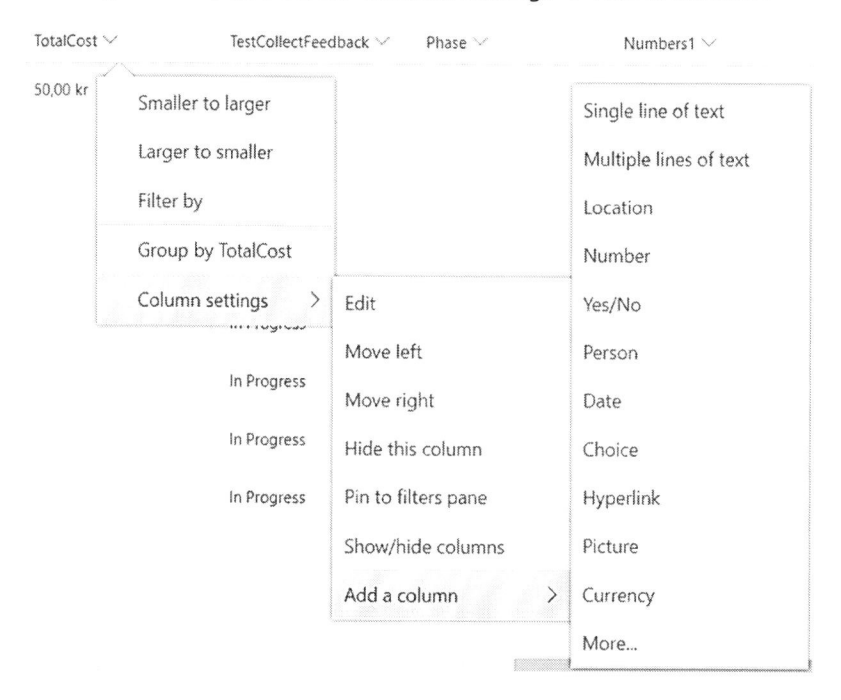

3.6.2 Character Limits in Text Columns

SharePoint apps have two text columns: Single line of text and Multiple lines of text. One line can only have 255 characters, so the Single line column is limited to that.

For the 'Multiple lines of text' there are two ways to give more space.

- When the 'Multiple lines of text' column is created in the "Create Column" page, there is a setting for number of rows. The default number is 6. This option is available for all apps. 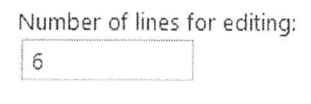
- **Library** apps have a setting in the right Edit column pane where you can allow unlimited length. This option is disabled by default.

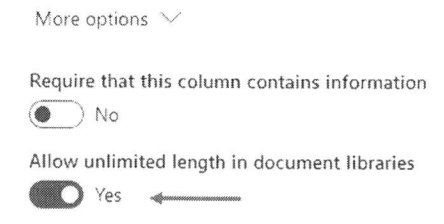

3.6.3 Column Types

As you have seen in the images above there are many column types. Here, I will just mention some of them that I think might need some extra explanation.

I will show the right pane options below. If you use the "Create Column" page, the options are similar.

3.6.3.1 Date and Time Column

Columns of the type Date and Time have a DateTimePicker at the Date field.

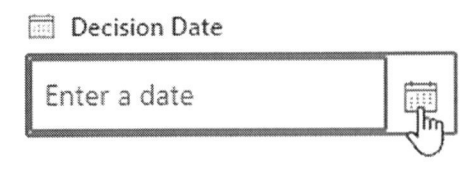

Decision Date

Enter a date

When you create a Date and Time column, you will have some options that are only available for this column type:

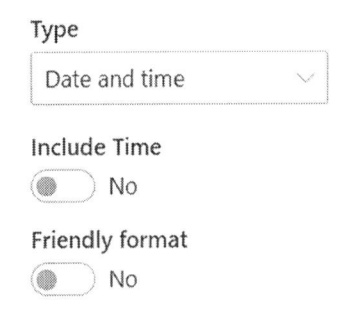

Type

Date and time

Include Time

No

Friendly format

No

If you change the Display Format from Standard to Friendly, the selected date will be shown like this:

Quote Date

Tomorrow

Thursday

3.6.3.2 Choice Column

When a column is of the Choice type, users who create a new item and fill out the metadata are asked to make a choice among several alternatives.

When you select the Choice column type, a right pane will open where you should fill out the choices in the order you want them to be shown.

It is usually recommended to enter the choices alphabetically, but another option is to add figures before the options, to indicate a proper order.

The choice options are given different colors, and you can change the colors by clicking on the palette icon. Remove the options with the X icon.

If you choose to set a default value, it will be filled out when no other value is selected.

Under 'More options' you can select display method for the choices. A dropdown menu is default, but when there are only a few options, it might be nice to have radio buttons instead.

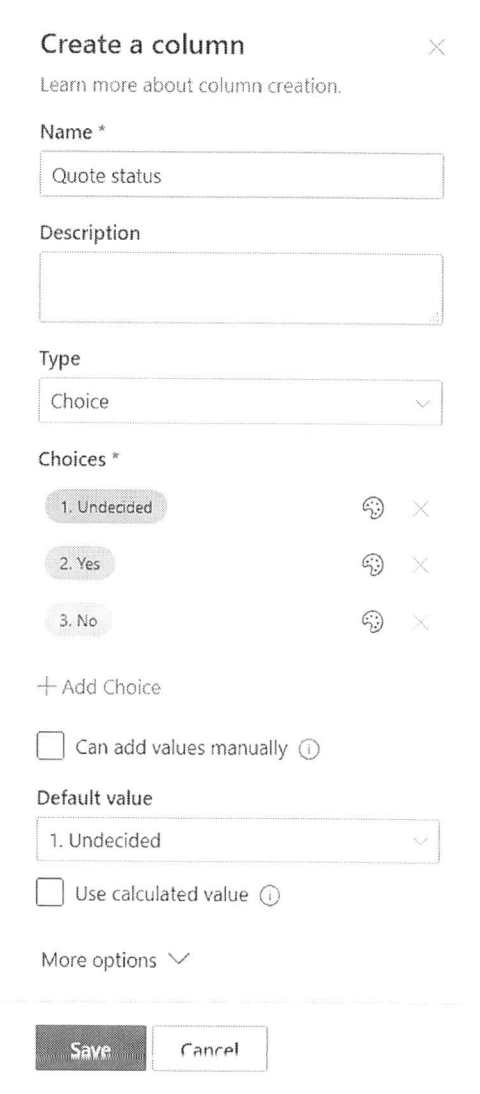

3.6.3.3 Location Column

The Location column type makes it possible to have location data from Bing Maps, or from your organization's directory, filled out automatically when a new item is created.

This column type is not possible to create from the app settings.

When you create a Location column, you can select which other location data columns should be filled out automatically. (By default, no boxes are checked.)

Think twice when you choose a name for the column, because if you change the column name, the connected location data columns will still have the original name.

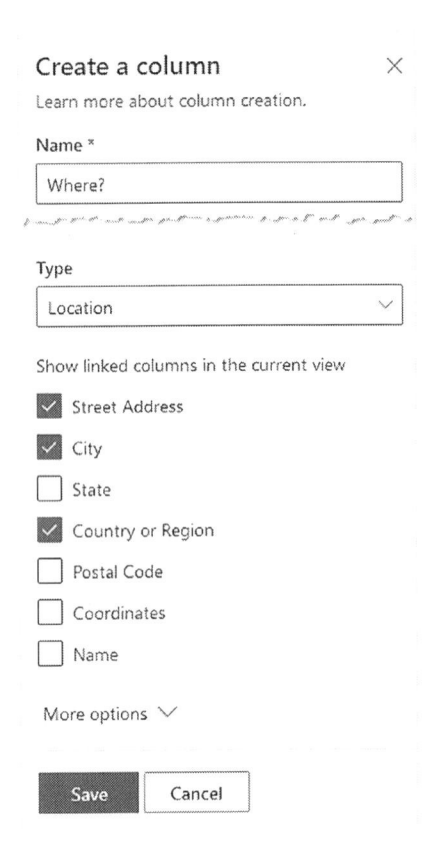

When a new item is created, users only need to select the location.

The other location details will be filled out automatically according to the column settings.

Where?	Where?: Street	Where?: City	Where?: Countr...
Eriksberg Hotel & Nature Reserve	Guöviksvägen 353	Trensum	SE

3.6.4 Edit a Column

If you want to make changes in the settings for an existing column, you can do that in two ways:

- In Standard view mode, columns can be moved, hidden and edited in other ways directly from the dropdown at the column. Select first 'Column settings' and then the modification you want to perform. The options are a bit different depending on column type.

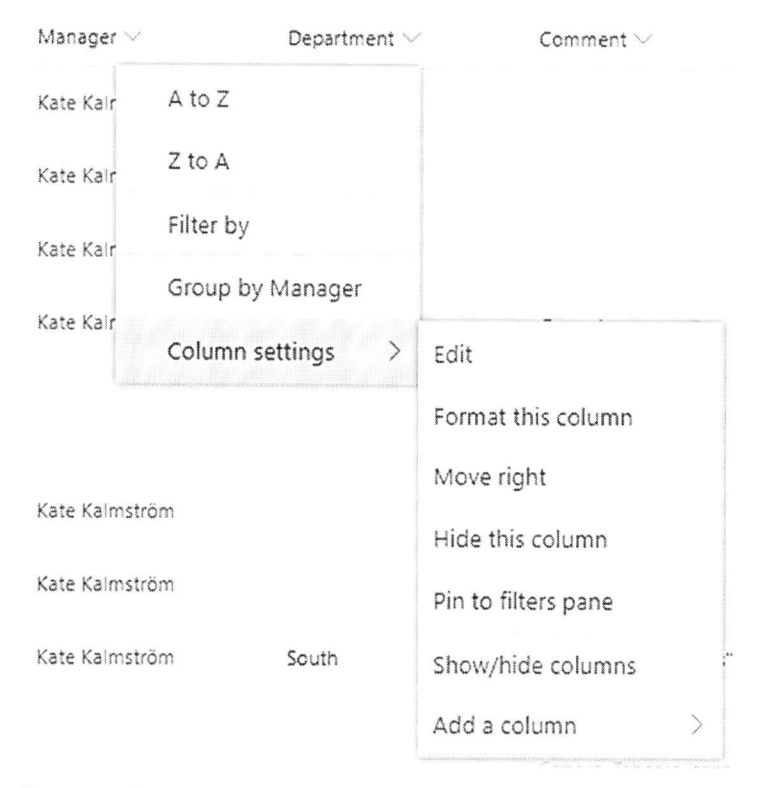

Manager ⌄	Department ⌄	Comment ⌄
Kate Kalr	A to Z	
Kate Kalr	Z to A	
Kate Kalr	Filter by	
Kate Kalr	Group by Manager	
	Column settings >	Edit
		Format this column
		Move right
Kate Kalmström		Hide this column
Kate Kalmström		Pin to filters pane
Kate Kalmström	South	Show/hide columns
		Add a column >

Some options open an Edit column right pane, where you can make your changes. Options like 'Move' and 'Hide' are performed immediately.

- Open the List or Library settings and find the Columns section. Click on the column you want to edit, and the 'Edit Column' page for that column will open.

Here you will have the same options as in the "Create Column" page, *see* above, except for the full column type selection. That is because switch of column type, can only be done under certain circumstances.

For some column types it is not possible to switch type at all. Other column types give such a possibility, but you cannot switch to any other type.

3.6.5   Edit Column Values

In the Grid view mode, you can edit the metadata of all app items by simply changing the values in the cells. In the Grid view mode, you can also drag a value in a cell down to the cells below, like you can do in Excel, *see* below.

In Standard view mode, you can edit the metadata in the Information pane >Edit all.

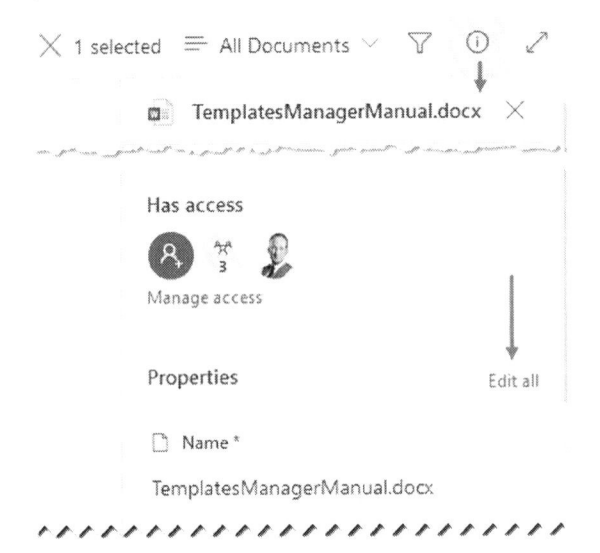

```
X  1 selected    ≡ All Documents ⌄    ▽    ⓘ    ↗
                                      ↓
              TemplatesManagerManual.docx    X


        Has access

         👤   👥   👨
              3
        Manage access
                                    ↓
        Properties                  Edit all

         📄  Name*

        TemplatesManagerManual.docx
```

3.6.5.1   Edit Multiple Items

There are two ways to edit multiple items at the same time. This is convenient when you want to give multiple items the same value in one or more columns.

- In the Grid view mode, drag the value in a cell down to the cells below.
- As the 'Edit' button in the command bar is visible when you select multiple items, you can edit multiple items in the Standard view mode right pane. The values you enter in the right pane will be applied to all selected items.

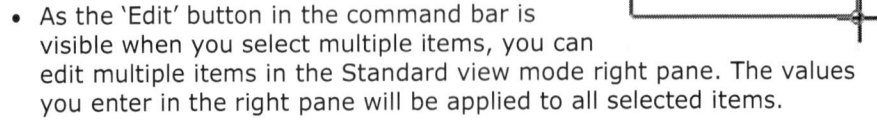

Sales

All columns that can be edited in the app are displayed in the right pane when you select multiple items and click on 'Edit' in the command bar. Of course, you only need to add a value in one of them – or in those columns that you want to change. The other columns will keep their current values.

The bulk edit feature is especially useful if you cannot sort the items in a way that makes it possible to drag down a value in the Grid view mode.

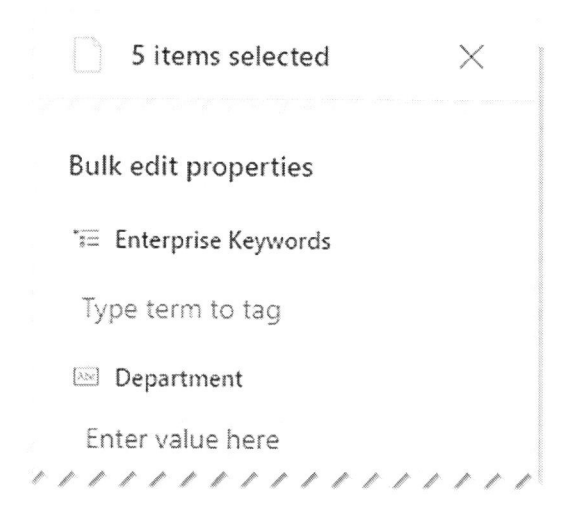

3.6.6 Filter, Sort and Group

SharePoint app items can be filtered by the various column values they contain. The column values can also be sorted ascending or descending, and you can combine filtering and sorting of several columns.

In general, app filtering works in the same way as in Excel and Access. A funnel icon to the right of the column name shows that a column has been filtered, so that it does not show all items.

The options to filter on are selected with check boxes in a right pane. In the image below, the Department column is ready to be filtered.

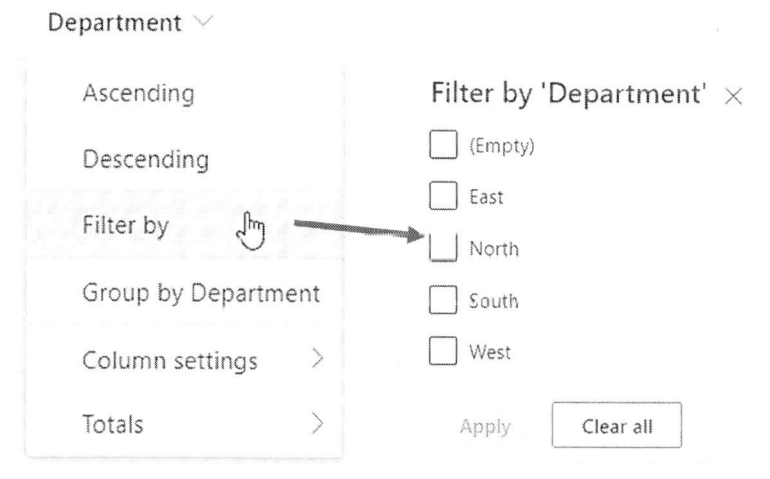

Check the boxes for the values you want to show and click on 'Apply'.

Uncheck boxes or click on 'Clear all' and then 'Apply' to remove the filter.

With the funnel icon in the right part of the command bar, you can filter multiple columns in an app at the same time.

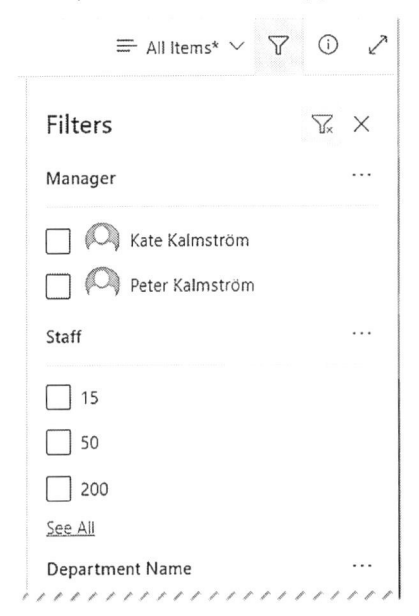

The Standard view mode also lets you group items by the values in one of the columns. In the image to the right, the "Manager" column has been grouped, so there is an icon to the right of the column name.

Click on the 'Group by' entry in the dropdown to remove the grouping.

There is no Grid option in the grouped view.

The filter, sorting or grouping is dynamically added to the URL, so you can link directly to a specific filter or sort option.

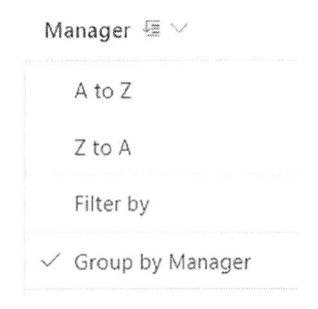

You can see this at the end of the URL. For example, "FilterField1%3D**Country**-FilterValue1%3D**Canada**" at the end of a URL shows that the Country column is filtered to only show items with the value Canada.

3.6.7 Format a Column

You can format columns with data bars and conditional formatting via Column settings >Format this column. You can also reach the column formatting options from the View selector, *refer to* 3.7.1, The View Selector.

36

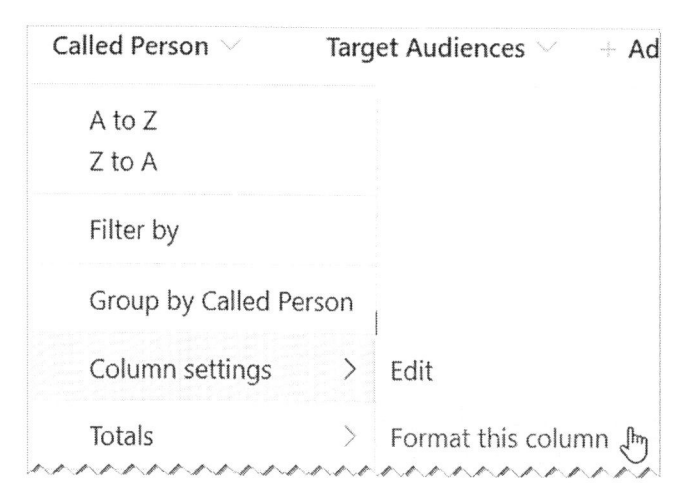

Called Person ⌄	Target Audiences ⌄	+ Ad
A to Z		
Z to A		
Filter by		
Group by Called Person		
Column settings >	Edit	
Totals >	Format this column 👆	

Number columns have the two options you can see in the image below, Data bars and Conditional formatting.

Date and Time columns have a Format dates option instead of Data bars.

Other column types only have the Conditional formatting option.

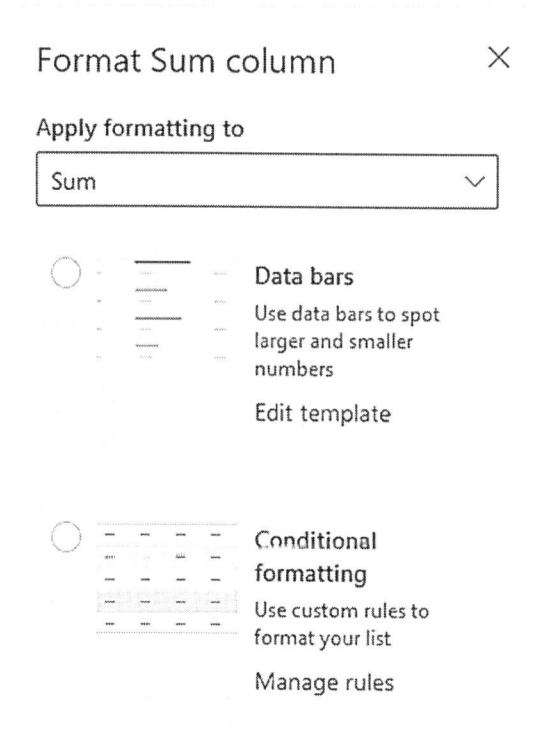

Format Sum column   ✕

Apply formatting to

[Sum ⌄]

○   **Data bars**
Use data bars to spot larger and smaller numbers

Edit template

○   **Conditional formatting**
Use custom rules to format your list

Manage rules

3.6.7.1 Data Bars

The Data bars formatting option can show different colors for positive and negative numbers in the column: The data bar size adapts to the number value.

You can also set a minimum and maximum number to format.

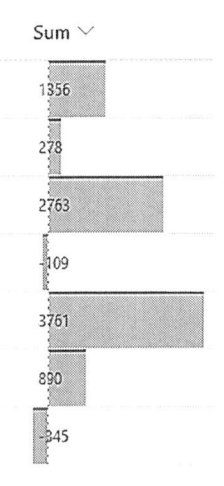

3.6.7.2 Conditional Formatting

The Conditional formatting option lets you create a rule – or a combination of rules for the column. In the image below I have selected to mark all values greater than 1000 with green color.

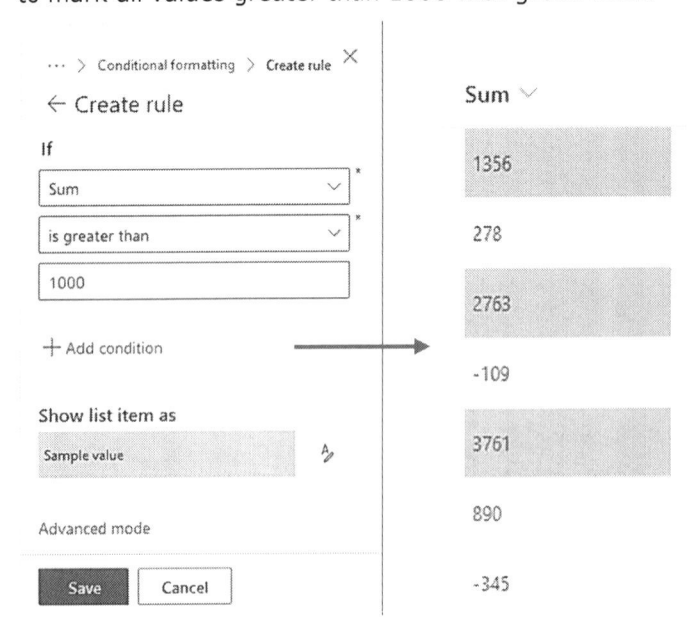

3.6.8 Rename a Column

You can rename all columns via the app settings. Just click on the column name to open the 'Edit Column' page and write another name in the 'Column name' field.

Columns can also be renamed directly in the app interface, via the column settings dropdown or in the Edit column right pane.

3.6.9 Edit the Form

The modern interface gives a possibility to decide which columns are displayed in the app form – that is, which fields users see when they fill out the properties of an item.

1. Select an item in the app.
2. Next step depends on if you want to modify a list or a library app:

- In a list app, open the Information pane for the selected item. At the bottom of pane, click on 'Edit columns'.

  (You can find the 'Edit columns' command in several places, but they require more clicks.)

- In a library app, click on 'Properties' in the command bar. Open the dropdown in the top right corner of the right pane and select 'Edit columns'.

  (Configure layout is out of scope for this book, and Power Apps is covered in chapter 21.)

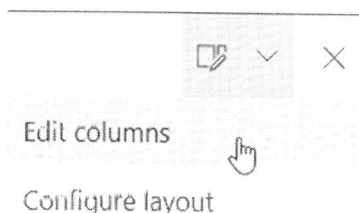

3. Uncheck the boxes for the columns you don't want to show in the form.

Edit columns in the form

Select a column to show or hide it in the form. To reorder columns, use drag and drop, or find more options next to each column. Required columns and columns with conditional formulas can't be hidden.

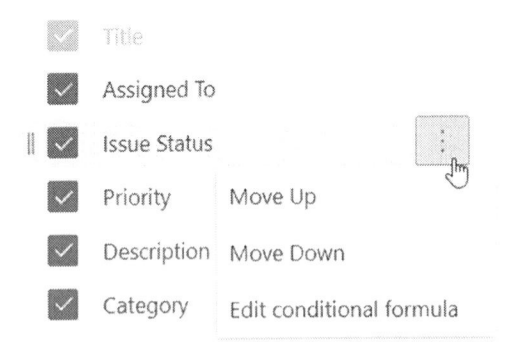

- ☑ Title
- ☑ Assigned To
- ☑ Issue Status
- ☑ Priority — Move Up
- ☑ Description — Move Down
- ☑ Category — Edit conditional formula

4. Move columns if needed, so that you get the fields in the preferred order.
5. Click on 'Save'.

Now all new and existing items will show only the checked columns as fields in the form, in the modern as well as in the classic interface.

Use views instead, *see* below, if you want to change how the columns are shown in the app interface.

3.7 VIEWS

All apps can show the data stored there in different ways. A view is a permanent way to display app items and properties, as opposed to the temporary ad-hoc filtering or grouping I described above.

There are two kinds of views: personal and public. The personal view is only shown to the person who created the view, while public views are shown to all users. The public view is the one I am referring to below.

The default view, created by SharePoint, is called "All Items" in list apps, "All Documents" in library apps and "Calendar" in calendar apps. These are basic views that show all items in the app.

When you have created an app and the columns you want to use, I would recommend that you also create some more views than the default one. When you combine meaningful views with the use of columns for relevant metadata, the information in your app can be sliced and diced in many ways, and your app will be very informative.

3.7.1 The View Selector

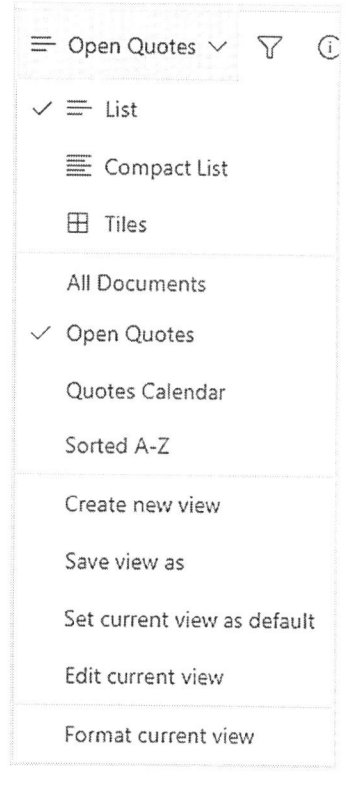

You can find all the app's views in the View selector to the right in the command bar. Only the name of the current view is displayed in the command bar. To see the other views, you must open the dropdown at the View selector.

Layout options:

Above the views, there are layout options. The 'List' option is default, but both list and library apps also have a 'Compact List' layout.

The third layout option is 'Gallery' in lists and 'Tiles' in libraries.

In Grid view mode, the default option is 'Autofit height', but there is also a 'Fixed height' option.

Create view:

The 'Create new view' link below the views in the View selector dropdown opens a dialog with a choice to show the data in the default list view or in a calendar view, *see* below.

To create a new view, you can also use the 'Save view as' option. This saves the current configuration of the page (for example the filter options) as a new view.

Set default view:

The command, 'Set current view as default', is shown when another view than the default view is selected. When you make a view default, all users will reach that view first, regardless of how they open the app.

The Grid view mode does not work in grouped views, so you should not make a grouped view the default view.

Edit view:

In the View dropdown, you can also find a link to editing of the current view.

Format view:

The last option 'Format current view' gives options that remind of the column formatting I described above. In views, the formatting options are conditional formatting and different colors on even and odd rows.

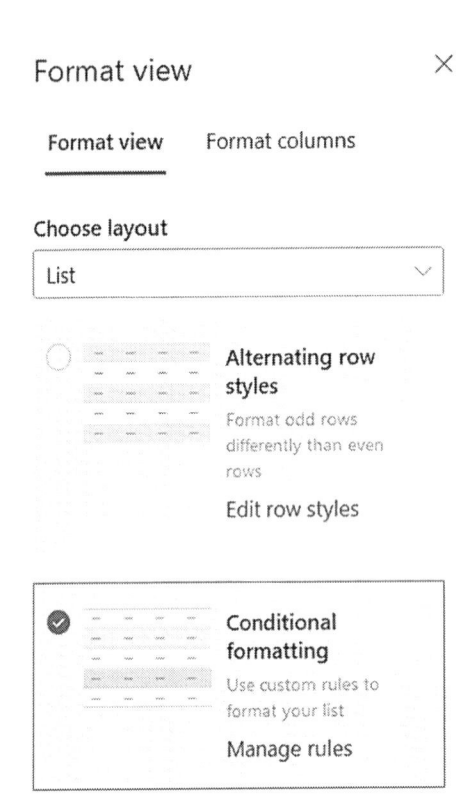

3.7.1.1 Create a New View

As we have already seen, you can create a new view by saving an existing filter and/or group option as a new view.

When you click on the 'Create new view' link under the View selector, a dialog opens. Here you can choose to show the data in the default list view or in a calendar view.

When you select to show the view as a list, you only need to enter a name.

When you choose the calendar option, you also need to specify which dates should be the start and end dates of the calendar and which column name should be displayed on the calendar "event".

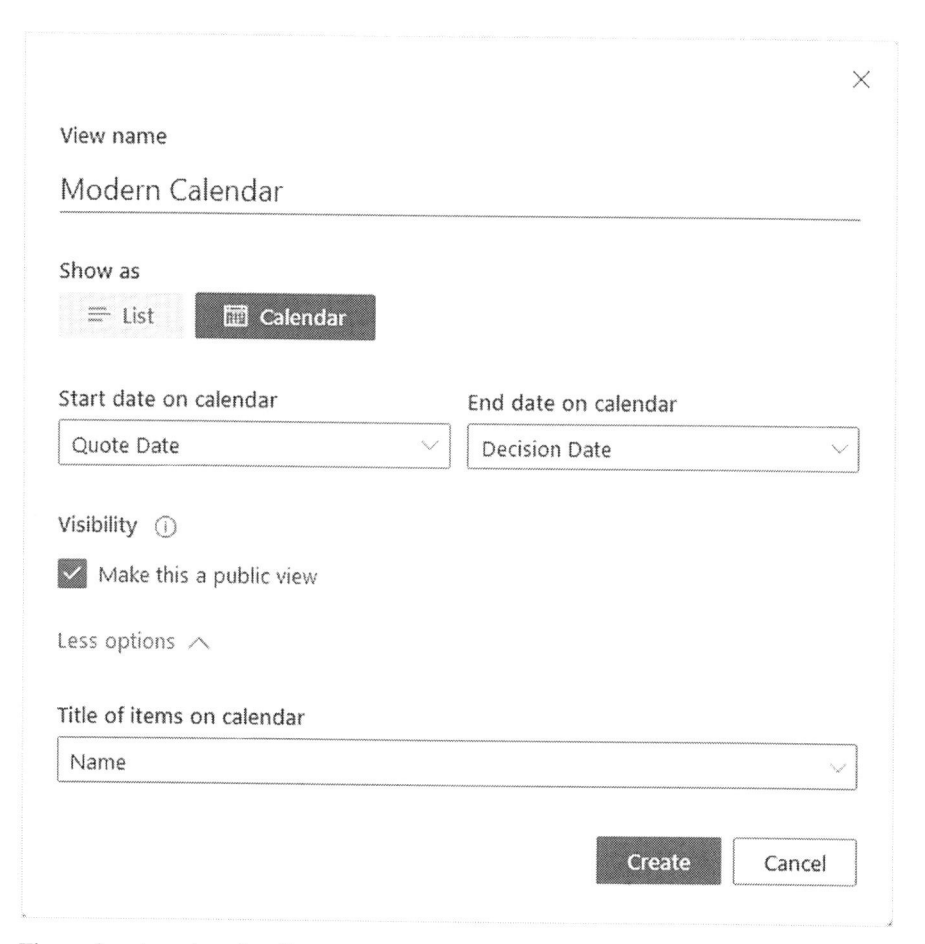

The calendar view is of course most suitable for lists where you actually want to show dates, but it is possible to use it for all apps.

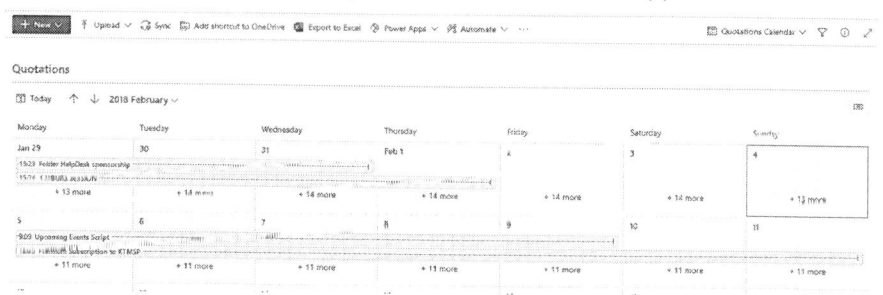

Another way to create a new view, is to open the List or Library settings and click on the 'Create view' link under the existing views.

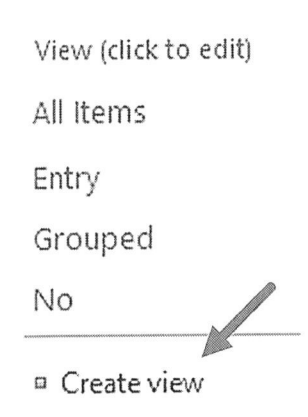

```
View (click to edit)

All Items

Entry

Grouped

No
           ↙
▫ Create view
```

That will direct you to a 'View Type' page, where you can select what kind of view you want to create.

In the 'View Type' page, you can also start from a view that already exists for the app and modify it.

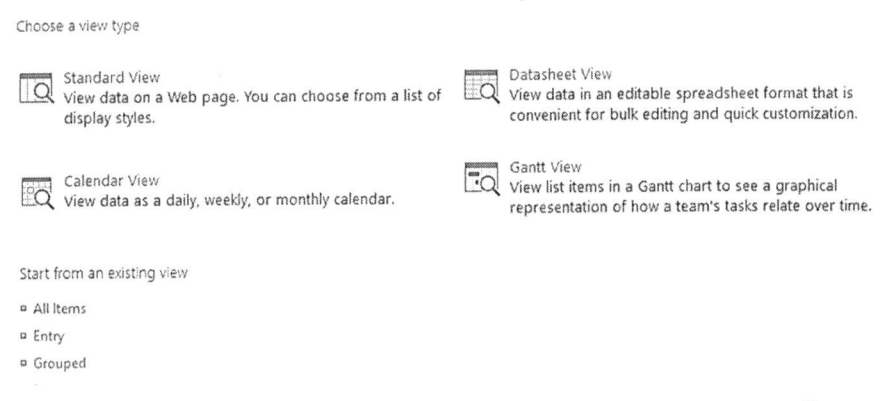

```
Choose a view type

    Standard View                                    Datasheet View
    View data on a Web page. You can choose from a list of    View data in an editable spreadsheet format that is
    display styles.                                  convenient for bulk editing and quick customization.

    Calendar View                                    Gantt View
    View data as a daily, weekly, or monthly calendar.    View list items in a Gantt chart to see a graphical
                                                     representation of how a team's tasks relate over time.

Start from an existing view

  ▫ All Items
  ▫ Entry
  ▫ Grouped
```

When you choose one of the four view type options, a "Create View'" page will open. It is a bit different for each view type, but it always reminds of the "Edit View'" page, *see* below.

When you modify an existing view by clicking on one of the views under 'Start from an existing view', the "Create View'" page will also open, but with the settings from the selected view.

3.7.2   Edit a View

To edit an existing view, you can:

- Click on the 'Edit current view' link in the View selector, *see* above.
- Open the List/Library settings and click on the name of the view you want to edit.

View (click to edit)
All Items
My Messages
New Phone Message

▫ Create view

In both cases, a new page will open where you can include/exclude and order columns, sort, filter and group the content and much more. (By default, the 'Columns', 'Sort' and 'Filter' sections are expanded when the page opens.)

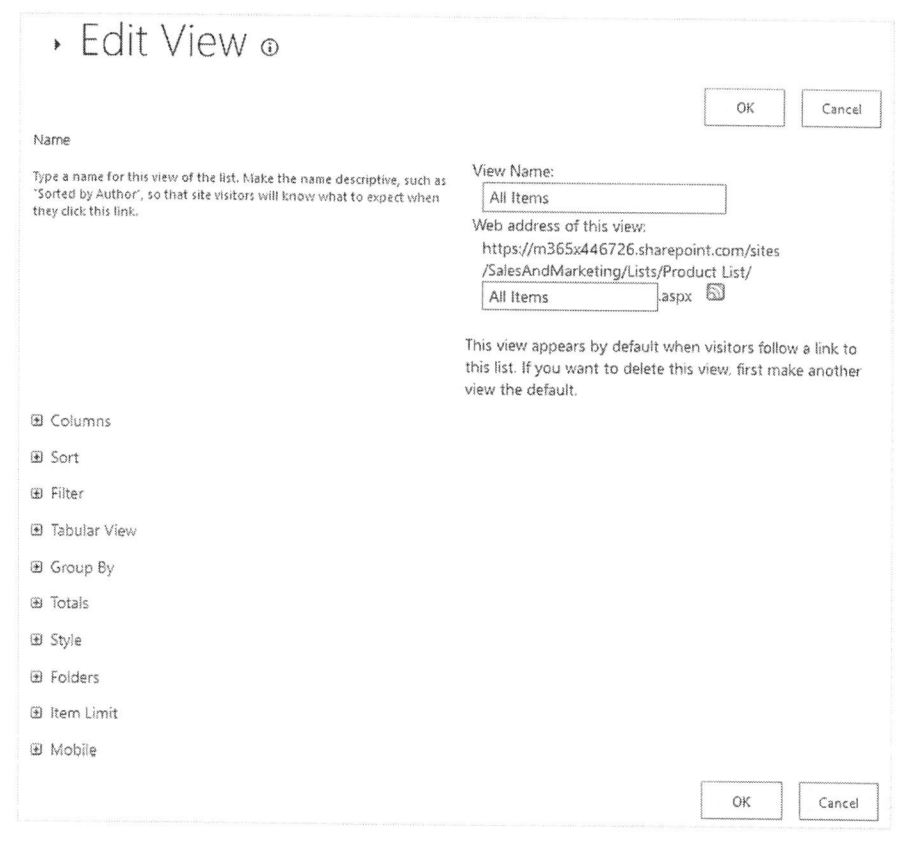

▸ **Edit View** ⓘ

OK   Cancel

Name
Type a name for this view of the list. Make the name descriptive, such as 'Sorted by Author', so that site visitors will know what to expect when they click this link.

View Name:
All Items

Web address of this view:
https://m365x446726.sharepoint.com/sites/SalesAndMarketing/Lists/Product List/
All Items .aspx

This view appears by default when visitors follow a link to this list. If you want to delete this view, first make another view the default.

⊞ Columns
⊞ Sort
⊞ Filter
⊞ Tabular View
⊞ Group By
⊞ Totals
⊞ Style
⊞ Folders
⊞ Item Limit
⊞ Mobile

OK   Cancel

The image to the right shows the upper part of the 'Columns' section. Of course, the column names are different in each app, depending on app type and how the columns have been created and modified.

Check the box for the columns you wish to show in the view and put them in the preferred order.

When you change the order number of one column, the others will adapt automatically.

Display	Column Name	Position from Left
☑	Title (linked to item with edit menu)	1
☑	Code Name	2
☑	Product Line	3
☑	Product Type	4
☑	Color	5
☑	Notes	6
☑	Enterprise Keywords	7
☐	App Created By	8
☐	App Modified By	9
☐	Attachments	10

The 'Filter' and 'Group by' options on this page gives a possibility to filter on a combination of values and to group on two levels.

Group By

Select up to two columns to determine what type of group and subgroup the items in the view will be displayed in. Learn about grouping items.

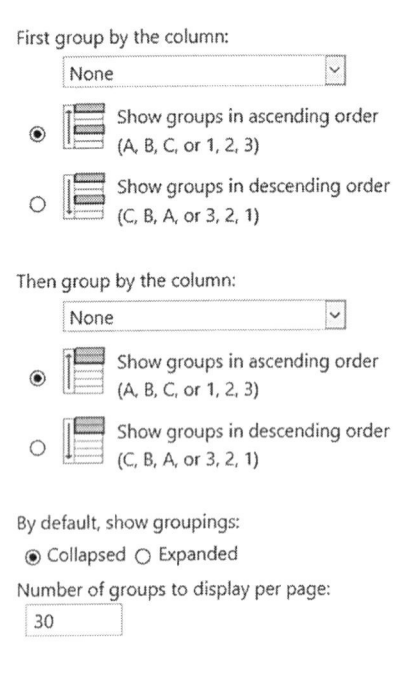

First group by the column:

None

● Show groups in ascending order (A, B, C, or 1, 2, 3)

○ Show groups in descending order (C, B, A, or 3, 2, 1)

Then group by the column:

None

● Show groups in ascending order (A, B, C, or 1, 2, 3)

○ Show groups in descending order (C, B, A, or 3, 2, 1)

By default, show groupings:

● Collapsed ○ Expanded

Number of groups to display per page:

30

3.7.2.1 Totals

The 'Totals' section in the Create View/Edit View page can be used to summarize the values in number and currency columns. You can only enable the Totals feature from the List/Library settings.

46

Computers

Title ⌄	Hardware Cost ⌄	Setup Cost ⌄
Kalle's laptop	$500	$100
Stina's tablet	$400	$50
Bert's desktop	$800	$200
	Sum $1,700	Sum $350

The 'Totals' feature can calculate sum and other numeric values, like average, maximum and minimum.

To add a Total to a column, scroll down to 'Totals' in the "Create View'" or "Edit View'" page and click on the plus sign to expand the 'Totals' section. Select the value you want to calculate from the dropdown to the right of the column that should have the Total.

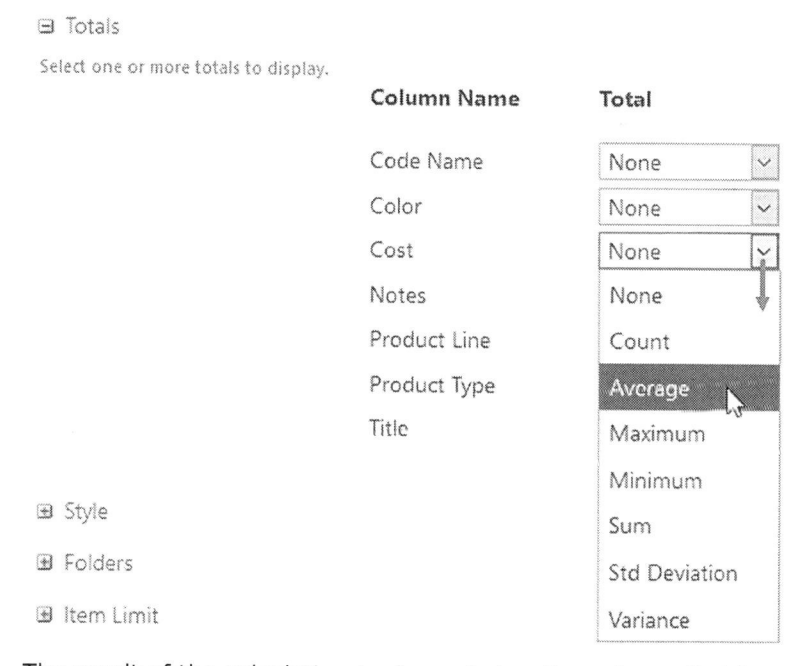

⊟ Totals

Select one or more totals to display.

Column Name	Total
Code Name	None
Color	None
Cost	None
Notes	None
Product Line	Count
Product Type	**Average**
Title	Maximum
	Minimum
	Sum
	Std Deviation
	Variance

⊞ Style

⊞ Folders

⊞ Item Limit

The result of the calculation is shown below the column that is calculated.

Totals can only be displayed in the Standard view mode. When this is written, it is not visible in the Grid view mode.

In columns of other types than number and currency, you can use the 'Totals' feature to count the number of items in a column.

3.8 ALERTS

SharePoint apps have an alert feature that sends e-mail notifications on changes in the app. It is possible to set alerts for changes in single items and files. You can also set an alert for changes in a whole list or library.

When you want to have an alert for changes in a single item, select the item and click on the 'Alert me' link under the item's ellipsis.

When you want to have an alert for changes in the app, click on the 'Alert me' link for the app under the ellipsis in the command bar. No item should be selected.

Under the ellipsis in the command bar, you can also edit or stop the alert and reach other apps you have access to and set alerts for them.

⋯

🔔 Alert me

📝 Manage my alerts

The alerts can be somewhat customized, because you can decide at what time they should be sent and for what changes.

1. Change the title (= e-mail subject) if you don't want to use the default: app name (+ item).

2. If you are a Site administrator, *refer to* 9.2, SharePoint Groups, you can add people who should get the alert. Otherwise, you can only set the alert for yourself.

   Only send me alerts when:
   ● All changes
   ○ New items are added
   ○ Existing items are modified
   ○ Items are deleted

3. If your organization has text messaging service set up, you can choose between having the alert by SMS or by e-mail. (This is not possible in all countries.) Otherwise, e-mail is the only option.

   Send me an alert when:
   ○ Anything changes
   ○ Someone else changes an item
   ○ Someone else changes an item created by me
   ○ Someone else changes an item last modified by me

4. Select at what changes you want to receive alerts.

   ● Send notification immediately
   ○ Send a daily summary
   ○ Send a weekly summary

   Time:

5. Select when you want to receive alerts.
6. Click OK.

You will now receive an e-mail confirming that your alert has been set up.

3.9 DELETE AND RESTORE APP CONTENT

You can delete and restore content that you have created yourself. Site admins and site owners can delete and restore other content too. Only apps and items can be restored – not columns and views.

3.9.1 Delete an Item

To delete an item, you can select the item and click on the 'Delete' button in the command bar, in both Standard and Grid view. You can delete one or multiple selected items at the same time.

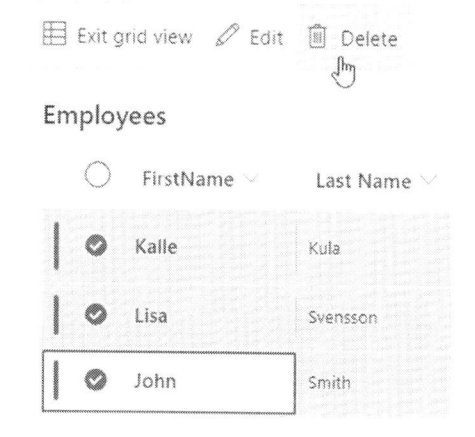

3.9.2 Delete a Column

There are two ways to delete a column:

- Open the column settings, *refer to 3.6.4, Edit a Column*, and select 'Edit'. A right pane will open, and it has a 'Delete' button at the bottom. 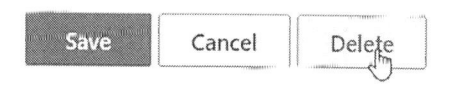
- Open the List/Library settings and find the list of columns. Click on the column you want to delete to open the 'Edit Column' page. Then click on the 'Delete' button at the bottom of the page.

Note that some columns are required and cannot be deleted, for example the "Title" column. If you don't need such a column, you can rename it and use it for something else that requires the same column type. (The "Title" column is a Single line of text column.)

3.9.3 Delete a View

You can find the Delete button for views if you click on the view in the Lis/Library settings, *refer to* 3.7.2, Edit a View. If the view is default, you cannot delete it until you have set another view as default.

3.9.4 Delete an App

To delete an app, open the List/Library settings and click on the link 'Delete this list' or 'Delete this document library' under the 'Permissions and Management' heading.

You can also open the Site contents, click on the ellipsis at the app you want to delete and select Delete.

In both cases, you will be asked to confirm that you want to delete the app.

3.9.5 Restore Deleted Content

Deleted apps and items are stored in the 'Recycle bin' library for 93 days. All users can see and restore content they have deleted themselves, and Site admins can see and restore all deleted content.

You can reach the Recycle bin from the Site contents. There is a button in the right end of the Site contents command bar.

In the recycle bin, you can either restore the selected content or delete it. There is also a button to empty the recycle bin of all content.

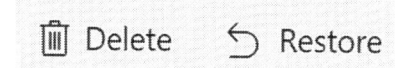

🗑 Delete   ↺ Restore

If you delete many document library files within one hour, SharePoint will send an e-mail with an option to restore the files.

3.9.5.1 Second-Stage Bin

Content that is deleted from the recycle bin, and content that has been in the recycle bin for 93 days, is not permanently deleted. Instead, it is moved to the second-stage recycle bin, where it is kept for another 93 days.

The link to the second-stage bin is found in the recycle bin page, but only the Site admin can see the link and restore or permanently delete content from the second-stage bin.

> Can't find what you're looking for? Check the Second-stage recycle bin

3.10 VERSION HISTORY

The SharePoint Version history, or Versioning, makes it possible to see and restore earlier versions of items in a list app and files in a library app. Version history is always set for the whole app, so that it applies to all the items contained in the app.

Version history is enabled by default when a new SharePoint document library is created. In other SharePoint apps, the Version history is disabled by default, but I recommend that you make it a habit to always enable the Version history when you have created a new app.

The Version history settings are managed in the List/Library settings >Versioning settings.

General Settings

- List name, description and navigation
- Versioning settings ⬅
- Advanced settings

3.10.1 See Version History

To see the version history, select the item, click on the item ellipsis and select 'Version history'.

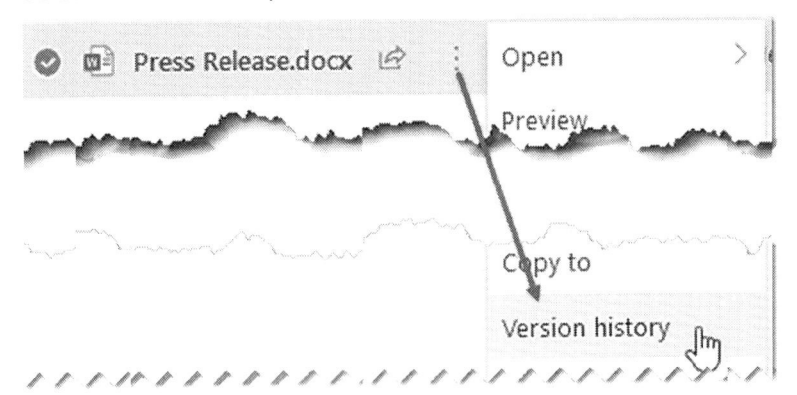

In calendars, select or open an event and click on the 'Version History' button under the EVENTS tab.

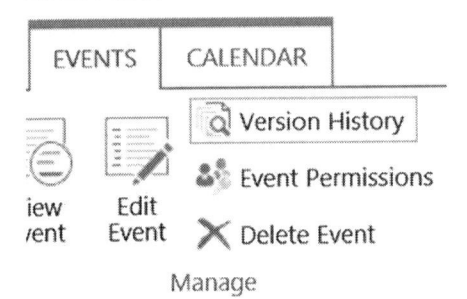

The Version history commands open a page that looks the same for library files and list items. Here, each version has a number and a date and time when the item was modified.

From the dropdown at the date, you can view the item properties, restore the item or delete it. (The current version cannot be deleted here.)

The image below shows the version history for a document library item that has six versions.

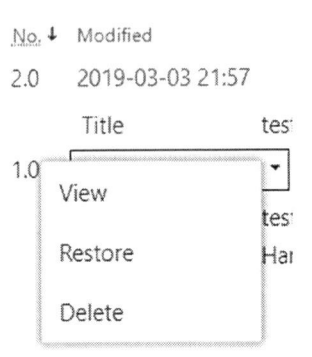

Delete All Versions

No. ↓	Modified		Modified By
6.0	2016-03-30 08:38		Kate Kalmström
	Description	Update the slideshow for the new version	
	Comments	It looks fine now. Thanks!	
5.0	2016-03-29 14:10		Rituka Rimza
	Comments	I added two slides about TimeCard Mobile and one about the Summary web part. Please have a look.	
4.0	2016-03-29 11:53		Kate Kalmström
	Comments	Yes, you are right. Please add them.	
3.0	2016-03-29 11:36		Rituka Rimza
	Comments	Done. How about TimeCard Mobile? Shouldn't we have 1-2 slides for the app too?	
2.0	2016-03-26 17:35		Kate Kalmström
	Task Name	TimeCard for SharePoint Slideshow	
	Description	Update the slideshow for the new version	
	Start Date	2016-03-26	
	Responsible	Rituka	
	Project	Other	
	Comments	Remember to include one slide with the TimeCard Summary web part.	
1.0	2014-11-13 12:40		Sales, kalmstrom.com
	Task Name	Slideshow	
	Priority	(2) Normal	
	Status	Not Started	
	Description	Update the slideshow with new images	
	Start Date	2014-10-20	

3.10.2 Version History in Library Apps

Office, image and PDF files are opened in the earlier version when you click on the date and time on the Version History page in a document library. Files that cannot be opened are downloaded.

To see the properties of an earlier version, click on the arrow at the date and select 'View'.

When you open an earlier version of an Office file, it has a Restore button below the ribbon.

Word files can be both restored and compared to other versions.

Compare   Restore

3.10.3 Version History in List Apps

When you click on the date and time on the Version History page in a list app, or if you select 'View' under the dropdown, the item properties are shown and the item can be directly restored or deleted.

3.11 SUMMARY

With this chapter, I wanted to give an overview over how you can create and edit SharePoint apps and use them to share information in an efficient and user-friendly way.

I hope you now understand how important it is to create suitable columns for metadata in apps and how you can filter and sort data in various ways and create different views. You should also know how to edit the app form, how to use versioning and alerts and how to delete and restore SharePoint apps and their content.

In the next chapter, we will take a closer look at the features that are specific for list apps. I will also describe two app types that are a bit different: the Tasks list and the Calendar.

4 LIST APPS

In the previous chapter, we looked at features that are common for all SharePoint Online apps. Now, we will go into features that only exist in list apps, and in the next chapter, we will do the same with library apps.

The main difference between list apps and library apps is that you use library apps to store and share files. List apps are used to store and share other data (even if you can attach files to them), for example data about departments, issues, staff or tasks.

When new list items are created, metadata info is added to fields in a form. Each field represent a column. When the form is saved, the values added to the form fields are displayed under the column headings in the app interface. *See* 4.4. below for details on how to create a new list item.

4.1 COMMAND BAR BUTTONS

As you already know, most apps can have two interfaces, modern and classic. A notable exception is lists built on the Tasks template, which only can be used with the classic experience. I will come back to the Tasks list at the end of this chapter. Now, I will first describe how the command bar in a modern list app can look and work.

The buttons in the modern experience command bar varies depending on the selection in the list of items, so that only relevant buttons are visible.

The image below shows the modern command bar in Standard view mode. The Grid view looks the same, except that 'Edit in grid view' is replaced by 'Exit grid view'.

4.1.1 No Item Selected

When no item has been selected in the list app, the command bar shows buttons to create new items, edit the list in grid view, share the list, export the list to Excel, create a powerapp from the list or create a flow that automates a process in the list.

Under the ellipsis, you can find the controls for alerts, *refer to* 3.8, Alerts.

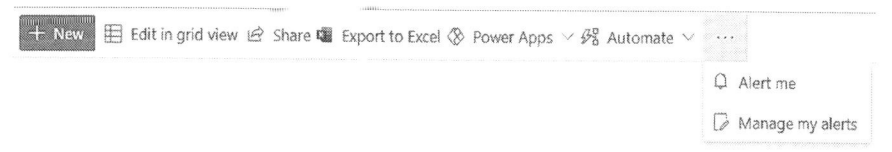

+ New   ⊞ Edit in grid view   ⌇ Share   ⤢ Export to Excel   ⊗ Power Apps ∨   ⚙ Automate ∨   ···

  🔔 Alert me

   ✎ Manage my alerts

I will come back to the 'Share' and 'Automate' commands in later chapters. PowerApps is out of scope for this book.

4.1.1.1 Export to Excel

When you click on the 'Export to Excel' button, the current view will be saved to Excel. In Excel, you can take advantage of the analysis, calculation and visualization features where Excel shines.

Different browsers give different options, so I have put parentheses around steps that are not available in all browsers.

1. In the SharePoint list, click on the 'Export to Excel' button in the command bar.
2. Download the file to your computer, or open it directly in Excel Online.
3. Click on 'Enable' on the warning message.
4. (Log in to 365 again.)
5. (Select how you want to view the data in Excel. The default option, Table, is often the most useful. If there is no choice, the list opens as a table.)

All the columns of the SharePoint view that you export will be included and visible in Excel. You will also have two extra columns, Item Type and Path, which you will probably want to hide.

When you have exported list data to Excel in this way, you need to make any changes in the SharePoint list, to have them reflected in the Excel file. It does not work the other way around.

4.1.2 One Item Selected

When one item has been selected, the command bar has no 'Export to Excel' or 'Power Apps' commands.

Instead, there are new commands for Edit, Copy link, Comment and Delete, and under the ellipsis we can now also find a command for Version history, if that has been enabled for the list.

+ New ⌀ Edit ▦ Edit in grid view ⇱ Share ⧉ Copy link ⊡ Comment 🗑 Delete ⅋ Automate ⌄ ⋯

                                                                                                      ⧉ Version history
                                                                                                       ◯ Alert me
                                                                                                      ▷ Manage my alerts

4.1.2.1 Edit

The 'Edit' command opens a right pane where the values in the various columns can be edited. To the right of the edit form, there is a comments field, *see* below.

In the Standard view mode, you can also click on the item's "Title" value to open it and then click on 'Edit item' above the form.

Instead of comments, you can open the dropdown in the 'Comments' pane and select to show all activity for the item.

In the Grid view mode, you can edit the metadata of a list item by simply changing the values in the cells.

4.1.2.2 Comment

List apps give a possibility to comment on items. When you select an item and click on the 'Comment' button, the item will open in a right pane. It looks the same as the Edit pane, *see* the image above, but the form is not in edit mode. Instead of the 'Save' button, there is an 'Edit all' button.

The "'Comments' pane gives a thread of unformatted comments, with information on who made the comment and when the comment was entered.

You can also see a comments icon to the right of the first column in a selected item. If there is a comment on the item, the icon has three dots. If there is no comment, the icon is empty and has a plus sign.

When you click on the icon, the same right pane opens as when you click on the 'Comment' button in the command bar.

4.1.2.3 Copy Link

The 'Copy link' command opens a dialog where you can copy the link and decide what people who have access to the link should be allowed to do with it.

Note that the default permission is very generous. It allows every person that gets access to the link to edit your item. Click on the default option if you want to change what people can do. We will come back to sharing and permissions in chapter 9.

4.1.3 Multiple Items Selected

When multiple items have been selected, there are only commands for Edit, Edit in grid view and Delete.

4.2 CREATE A NEW LIST ITEM

The '+ New' button opens a right pane where the columns are displayed as fields. Now, you can fill out or select the values in the different columns/fields.

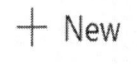

Some values might be there from the beginning, but in that case, they are often possible to change, if necessary.

In the image below, "Title" is marked with a star. That means that you must fill out a value in that field to be able to save the new item. There is always at least one such mandatory field in a list item, but it does not need to have the name "Title".

As you see, the "Returned?" field has a value already. Here, another value can be selected if needed.

> | Abl | Title *
>
> Enter value here
>
> 𝒬 Called Person
>
> Enter a name or email address
>
> ⊘ Returned?
>
> No
>
> | Abl | Who called?
>
> Enter value here

Lists in **Grid** mode have another option also: a blank row at the bottom of the grid. This last row is marked with '+ Add new item'. When you click on the text, the cells in the row become visible, so that you can create a new list item by entering or selecting values for each column.

+ Add new item

4.3 MICROSOFT LISTS

The Microsoft Lists app can be reached from the App Launcher in the top right corner of all Microsoft 365 apps. There is also a mobile app, currently only for iOS.

In Microsoft Lists, you can find all lists in the tenant that you have access to and have used recently – except for lists that only have the classic interface. There is a limit on 100 lists, and I have found that "recent" can be six months back if that limit is not exceeded.

The lists can be opened directly in Microsoft Lists, and except for the possibility to show the classic interface, they have the same functionality in Microsoft Lists as they have in SharePoint.

In Microsoft Lists, you can also create new list apps and add them to any site that you have access to.

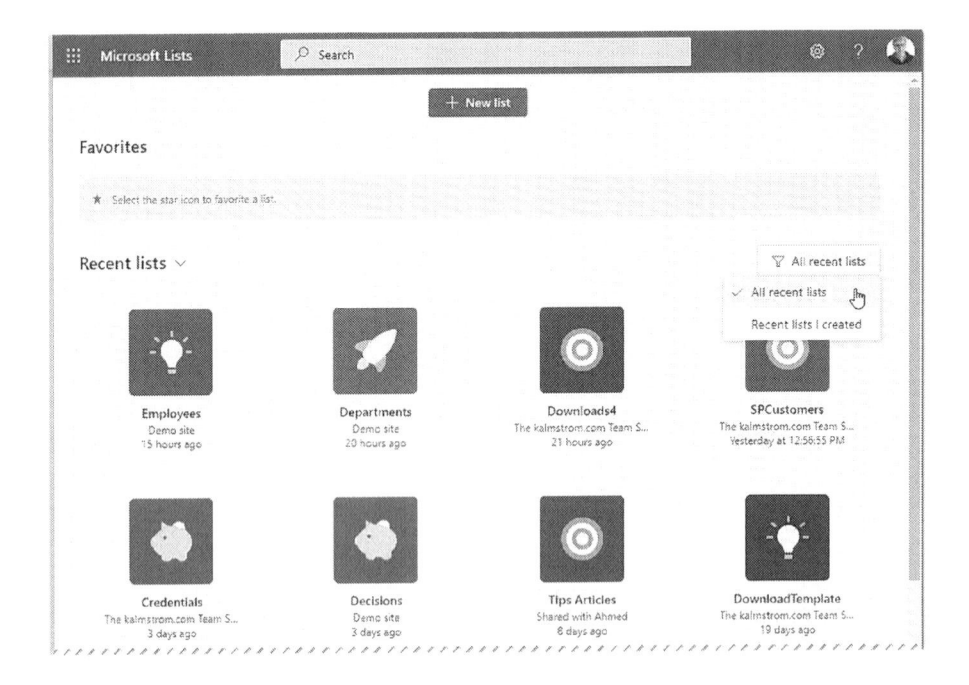

4.3.1 Create a New List App

You can always create a new list from the "Your Apps" page, as described in the previous chapter. Here, we will have a look at another option to create a list, that makes use of Microsoft Lists.

Apart from the 'App' link that takes you to the "Your Apps" page, the 'New' button in a modern SharePoint homepage or Site contents also gives the option 'List'.

When you click on the 'List' link, you will be directed to a limited version of Microsoft Lists. You cannot see all your other lists here, but you will have the same four list creation options as in the full version of Microsoft Lists:

- a blank list
- a list created from an Excel file
- a list created from an existing list
- a list created from a template.

The new list will be created in the current site, and it will open after creation.

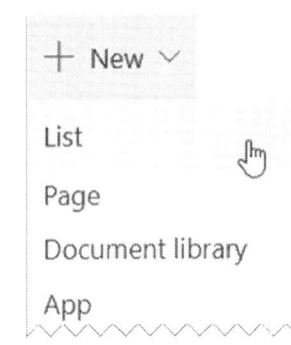

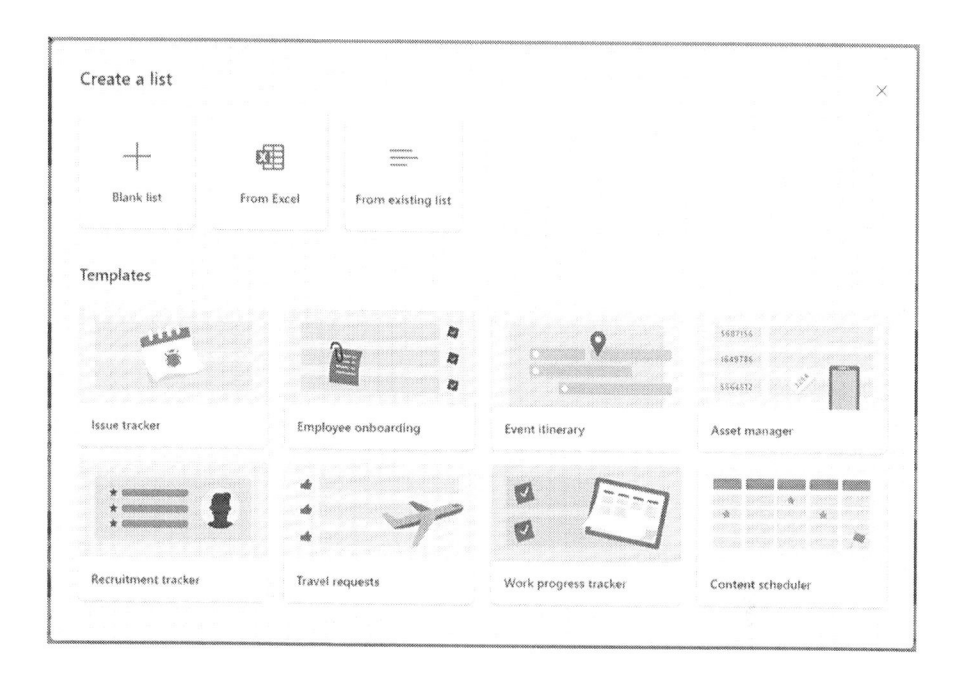

4.3.1.1 Blank List

When you select the 'Blank list' option, a custom list app with only a "Title" column will be created. Give the list a name and a description and click on 'Create'. (Uncheck the box, if you don't want to add a link to the list in the site's Site navigation.)

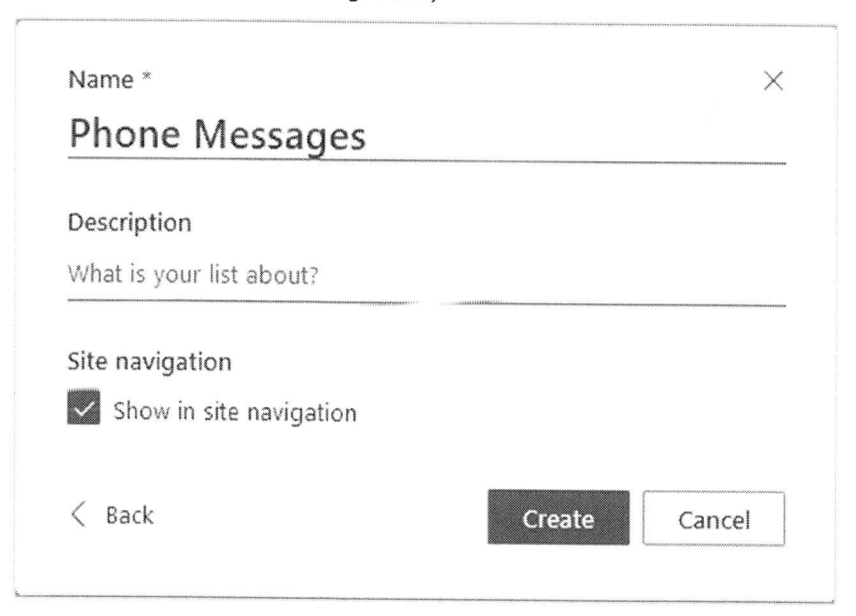

4.3.1.2 From Excel

Before you create a list from data in an Excel file, I recommend that you format the data you want to use as a table with no empty rows or columns. That will make the list creation easy.

The Excel file can be uploaded from your computer or selected from OneDrive for Business, *refer to* chapter 7.

After upload/selection of the file, you will have a possibility to change table – in case your file has multiple tables – and column types. You can also select to not include a column.

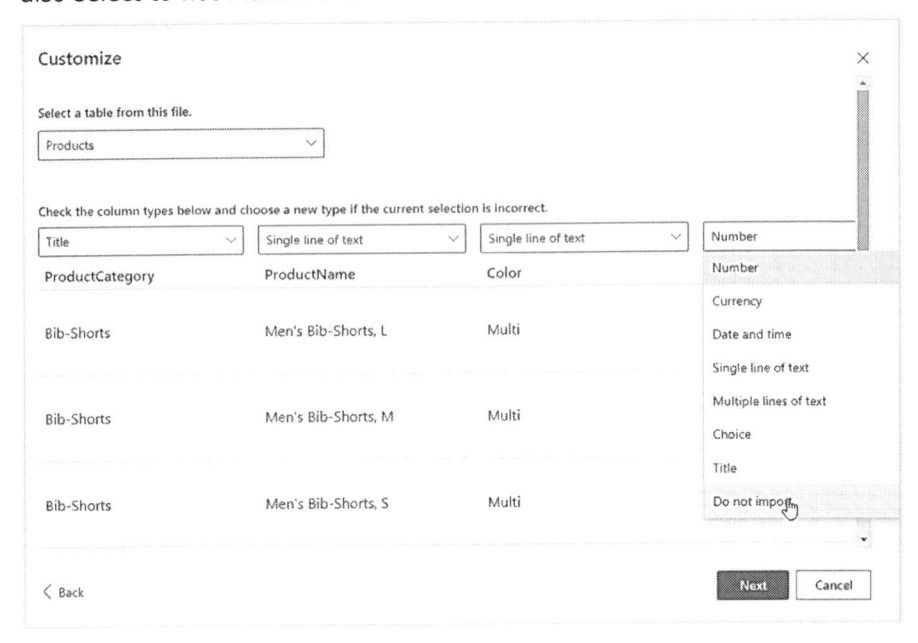

When you click on 'Next' you will have the same Name and Description options as when you create a list from blank.

Note that the new list is independent from Excel. There is no synchronization, so changes in one of the apps are not reflected in the other app.

4.3.1.3 From Existing List

When you create a list from an existing list, you can create a new list from any list that can have the modern interface and that you have access to. The new list will have the same columns, views and formatting as the original list. The items in the original list are not included.

[Screenshot: "Select an existing list" dialog showing Contoso team with lists: Content and Structure Reports, Marketing, Reusable Content]

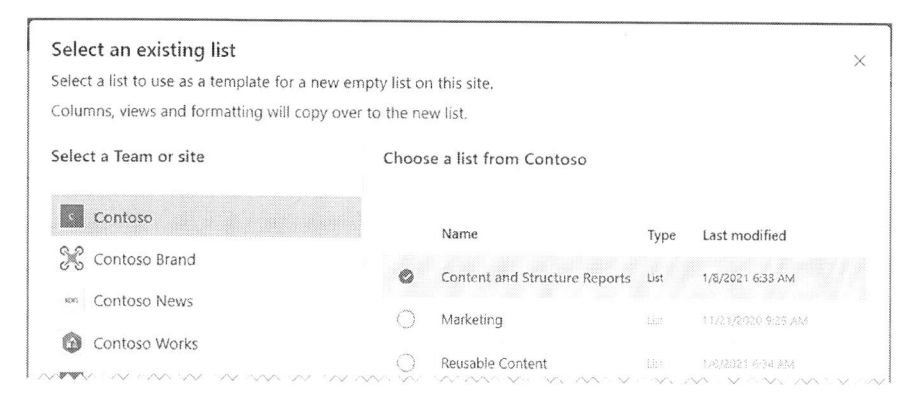

Select first site and then list app. When you have selected a list to create a new list from, you will have the same options as when you create a blank list.

4.3.1.4 From Template

Microsoft Lists gives some templates that you can create new lists from, but not as many templates as you can find on the "Your Apps" page.

However, all the Microsoft Lists templates take advantage of the 'Format this column' feature, which is not the case with the templates on the "Your Apps" page.

When you click on a template, a preview will open. If you change your mind after seeing the preview, you can select another template in the menu to the left.

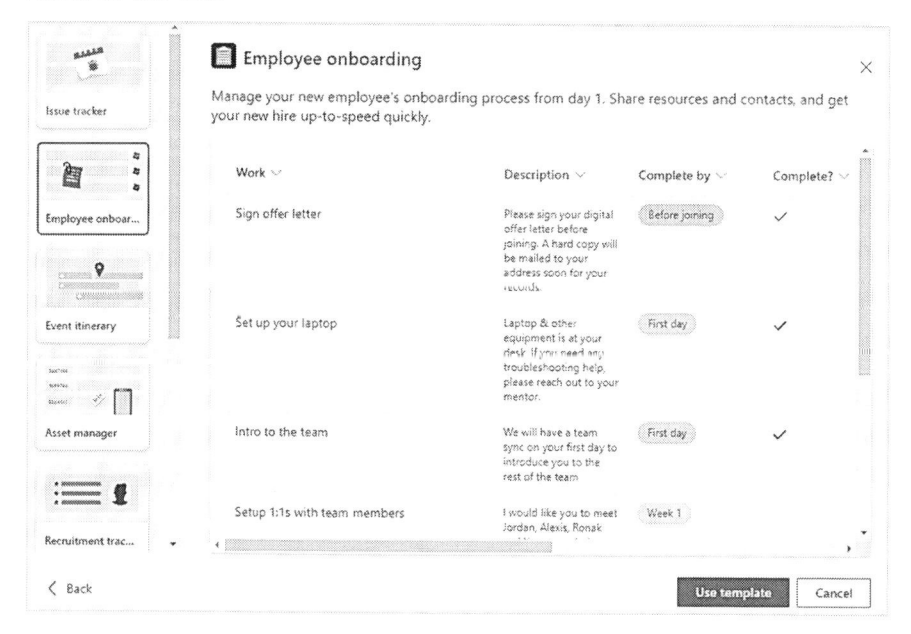

[Screenshot: Employee onboarding template preview showing columns Work, Description, Complete by, Complete? with sample rows: Sign offer letter, Set up your laptop, Intro to the team, Setup 1:1s with team members]

When you click on 'Use template', you will have the same options as when you create a blank list, but the new list will of course have all the columns, views and formatting of the template.

4.4 THE MULTI-LINE COLUMN

The column type Multiple lines of text (also called "multi-line column") has some features that are only available in list apps: rich text and append changes to existing text.

When you combine these two features, you can have a comments field with formatting that you can use instead of the 'Comment' command described above in 4.1.2.2.

4.4.1 Rich Text

When rich text is enabled in a Multiple lines of text column in a list app, it is possible to add formatting, tables, hyperlinks and images to the field when you create or edit the item.

A pen icon to the right of the column name in the edit pane shows that rich text has been enabled.

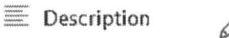

When you click on the pen icon, a new right pane will open where you can format the text.

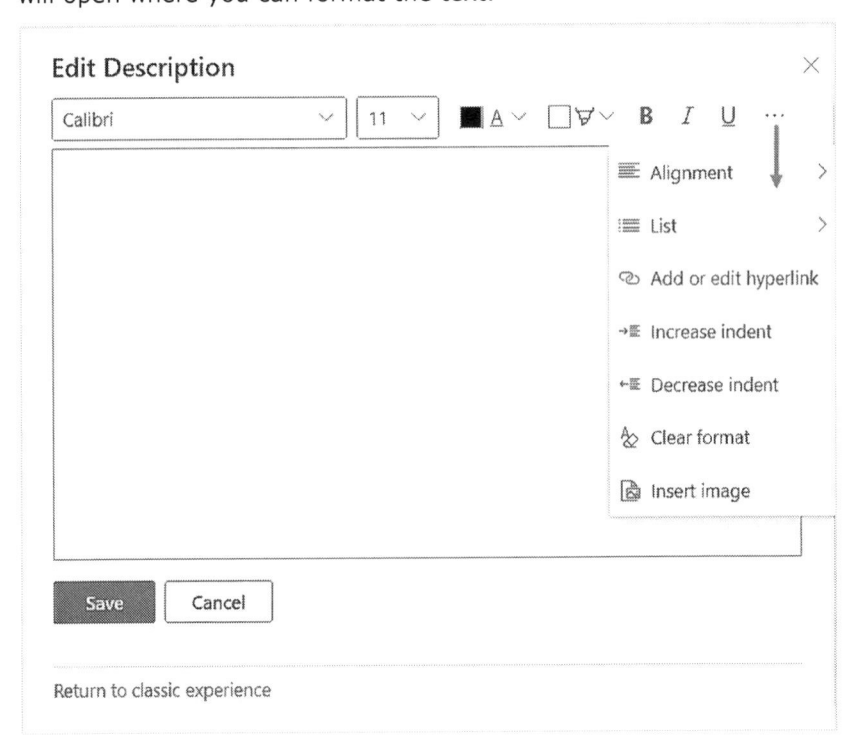

Should you need more options, click on the link to the classic experience. That opens yet another right pane, and when you click in the text field more options will open in the ribbon.

Remember to save your changes, under the EDIT tab in the classic ribbon or with the button at the bottom of the modern pane.

If the rich text feature is enabled by default or not depends on how you create the column:

- When you create a multi-line column from the '+ Add column' command in the modern interface, rich text is not enabled by default, but you can enable it under 'More options'.

  More options ∨

  Use enhanced rich text (Rich text with pictures, tables, and hyperlinks)
  ⬤ No

- When you create a multi-line column from the List settings 'Create column' dialog, rich text is enabled by default. If you only want users to add plain text, you must change the setting.

  Specify the type of text to allow:
  ○ Plain text
  ◉ Enhanced rich text (Rich text with pictures, tables, and hyperlinks)

4.4.2 Append Changes to Existing Text

In list apps, columns of the type 'Multiple lines of text' have a feature called 'Append changes to existing text'. It reminds of the Version history feature I described in 3.10, and to use this feature you must first enable Version history in the list.

There is however an important difference between Version history and Append changes: you cannot see the version history when you open an item – you must open the Version history to see it.

If you want to see the history for a 'Multiple lines of text' column as soon as you open the item, you should enable the 'Append changes to existing text' for that column. When you do that, all changes are shown as a thread in the 'Multiple lines of text' field.

The earlier text cannot be changed, but new text is shown above the earlier text in the field. The image below shows the same item as in the Version history section, see 3,10, but here comments from different versions are shown in the "Comments" field as a part of the open item.

Comments   ☐ Kate Kalmström (2016-03-30 08:38):

It looks fine now. Thanks!

☐ Rituka Rimza (2016-03-29 14:10):

I added two slides about TimeCard Mobile and one about the Summary web part. Please have a look.

☐ Kate Kalmström (2016-03-29 11:53):

Yes, you are right. Please add them.

☐ Rituka Rimza (2016-03-29 11:36):

Done. How about TimeCard Mobile? Shouldn't we have 1-2 slides for the app too?

☐ Kate Kalmström (2016-03-26 17:35):

Remember to include one slide with the TimeCard Summary web part.

The Append feature is especially useful for discussions and issue tracking.

4.4.2.1 Enable Append

To enable the Append feature, you need to edit the column where you want to append changes and set the toggler to 'Yes' under 'More options' in the right pane.

You can also open the List settings, click on the column name and select the 'Yes' radio button for 'Append changes to existing text'.

More options

Use enhanced rich text (Rich text with pictures, tables, and hyperlinks)
◉ Yes

Append changes to existing text
◉ Yes

Append Changes to Existing Text
◉ Yes   ○ No

4.5   THE TASKS LIST

When you create a list that builds on the Tasks list template, you will get a list with a classic interface that has most commands in the ribbon above the tasks. The Tasks list has some special features that are not available in other list apps with the classic interface:

- A timeline above the list of tasks.

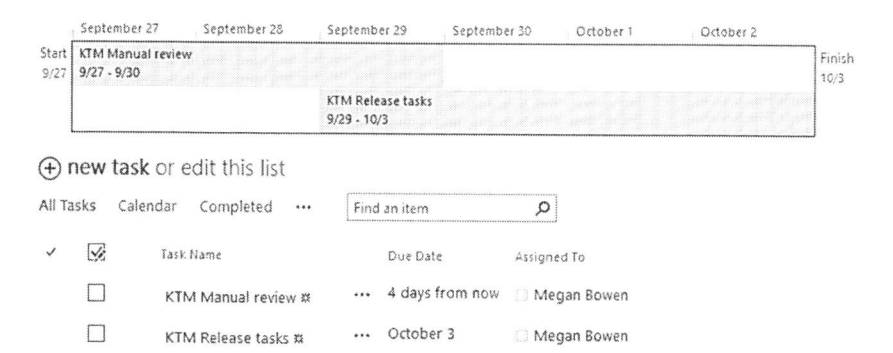

- Time related commands in a TIMELINE tab in the ribbon. Click on the timeline to show this tab.

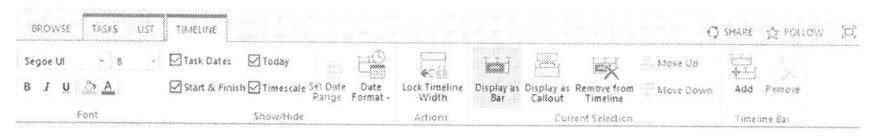

- A TASKS tab instead of the ITEMS tab.
- The default view is called 'All tasks'.

When this is written, the Tasks list can only be used with the classic interface, and because of that, you can only create it from the "Your Apps" page.

If you want to use the modern interface, I recommend the Issue tracker or Work progress tracker template instead. These templates are available in Microsoft Lists. There is also an Issue Tracking template created from the "Your Apps" page.

You should be aware, though, that these three options don't have a timeline and not as many other task tracking features as the Tasks list.

4.5.1 Tasks and Issue Tracking Alerts

SharePoint lists that build on the Tasks and the Issue Tracking templates have two alert possibilities that are not present in other apps:

- The Alert settings has a view selector under "Send me an alert when'.

  ◉ Someone changes an item that appears in the following view:
  My Issues ▼

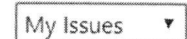

- Under 'Advanced settings' in the List settings there is a choice to send an e-mail to the person to whom a task has been assigned. The default value is 'No'.

E-Mail Notification
Send e-mail when ownership is assigned or when an item has been changed.

Send e-mail when ownership is assigned?

○ Yes   ● No

4.6 THE CALENDAR LIST

The calendar is a list type that has its own, classic interface. Use a SharePoint calendar to share event information like holidays, leaves, delivery dates and other information that is of common interest to the users who have access to the calendar.

A very common question is how SharePoint calendars relate/connect/interact with Outlook calendars. The short answer is that they do not. They are stored in totally different places, but SharePoint calendars also lack a range of important features that Outlook calendars have, such as invites, reminders and integration with Microsoft Teams.

On the other hand, the SharePoint Calendar app has more features than the calendar list view that I described in section 3.7.1.1, Create a New View.

To create a SharePoint calendar, add an app built on the Calendar template from the "Your Apps" page.

4.6.1 Calendar Views

By default, a calendar list displays a "Calendar" view that shows all events in a calendar-like interface. The "Calendar" view can display the events for a Day, Week or Month.

In the "Calendar" view, you can switch between periods with arrows.

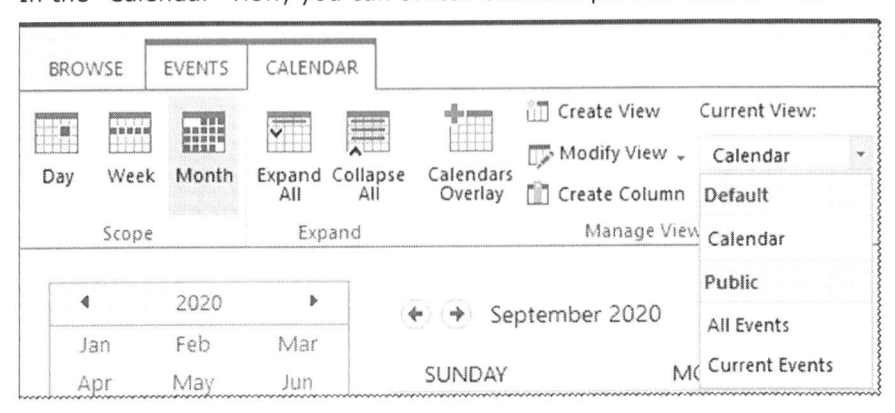

There are two more built-in views, "All Events" and "Current Events". Both these views show the events in the classic SharePoint list interface.

These views are suitable for editing of many events at the same time, as they have the 'Quick Edit' button that is missing in the "Calendar" view.

You can create more views from the List settings, in the same way as for other apps, and when you do that, you are given the "Calendar" view as one of the options.

4.6.2 Create a New Event

In the default "Calendar" view, new events are created with an '+ Add' link that is displayed when you hover the mouse cursor over a calendar date in the Month view or over an hour section in the Week and Day views.

You can also use the 'New Event' button under the EVENTS tab in the ribbon.

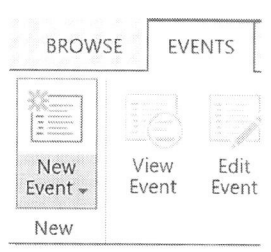

In other views than the calendar views, new items are created with a '+new' button.

4.6.3 Edit an Event

Use the 'Edit Event' button in the ribbon to open a selected event in edit mode.

You can also double-click on the event to open it and then click on 'Edit Item' in the ribbon of the open event.

4.7 SUMMARY

In this chapter, we have studied some features that are specific for list apps. You have been introduced to Microsoft Lists, and you know how to create list apps with the 'List' command.

We have also seen how you can create, edit and comment on list items, and I have described the list features 'Rich text' and 'Append to existing text'. Finally, we have looked at a few lists with special features: Tasks, Issue Tracking and Calendar.

Now it is time to have a look at the library apps.

5 LIBRARY APPS

A SharePoint library is an app with some unique qualities and features, and in this chapter, we will have a look at these.

What distinguishes libraries from other apps, is that each library item, or row, has a column that contains a file, and the other columns has metadata related to that file.

Some of the columns are built-in, such as 'Created' and 'Modified By', and their metadata is filled out automatically. You can, and should, also create your own, custom columns.

There are several types of SharePoint libraries, for example:

- Document libraries, mostly used for Office documents but can be used for other files as well
- Form libraries, used for forms
- Page libraries, used for custom SharePoint pages
- Picture libraries. used for images

These and more library types can be created from the "Your Apps" page.

A document library called "Documents" is created automatically, along with some other libraries, when you create a new site.

Here, I will focus on SharePoint document libraries, and when I write "library" in this book, I refer to a document library if nothing else is mentioned.

In this chapter, I will explain why using SharePoint document libraries is a good way to store and share information. You will also learn how to:

- Create content directly in a document library
- Upload files to a document library in various ways
- Work with files in a document library
- Check out and check in documents
- Manage file properties
- Copy and move files
- Use various other library specific commands

5.1 Why Document Libraries?

Document libraries are often the best way to share files within an organization, and it is certainly much better than sending e-mail attachments. When you use SharePoint document libraries for file sharing you have everything in one place, and all who have been given permission can reach the files.

A SharePoint document library is however more than a place for file storage and sharing – it is also a place where you can work with the files and even create new files.

I would recommend that you use many document libraries, as a way of categorizing files. For example, if your site is made for sharing information about a new product, you could have these libraries:

- Suggested Specifications
- Supplier Contracts
- Design Sketches
- Radio Commercials

In these libraries you would of course have files. Those files are sometimes referred to as documents in the SharePoint user interface. You can download files from a document library to your computer and vice versa.

5.2 Library Unique Features

When you click on the ellipsis to the right of the file name in a document library in Standard view mode, you will have many options for what to do with the file.

The most used of these options are also displayed in the command bar. Document libraries can be used with both the modern and the classic interface.

SharePoint document libraries have the same features as lists, like alerts, Version history and filtering, but libraries also have some specific features that I will describe below.

Most of these library specific commands affect the file that is stored in the library item – not the whole item.

There are no specific library commands when multiple items are selected.

5.2.1   No Item Selected

When no item is selected in the library, the command bar has three specific buttons, in addition to the buttons that are available in all apps:

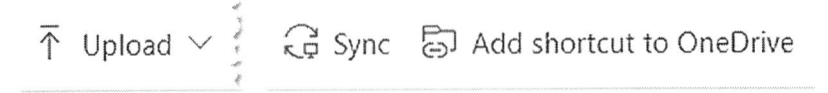

↑ Upload ⌄   ⇄ Sync   ⎘ Add shortcut to OneDrive

- Upload, for uploading files to the library. A new item for the file will be created automatically.
- Sync, to synchronize the library files with a folder on your computer, *refer to* 7.4, Synchronize with a Local Folder.
- Add shortcut to OneDrive, to add a shortcut to this library in the left menu of your default OneDrive for Business library, *refer to* chapter 7.

We will come back to these features later in the book.

5.2.2   One Item Selected

When one item is selected, there are more library specific features. We will come back to most of them later.

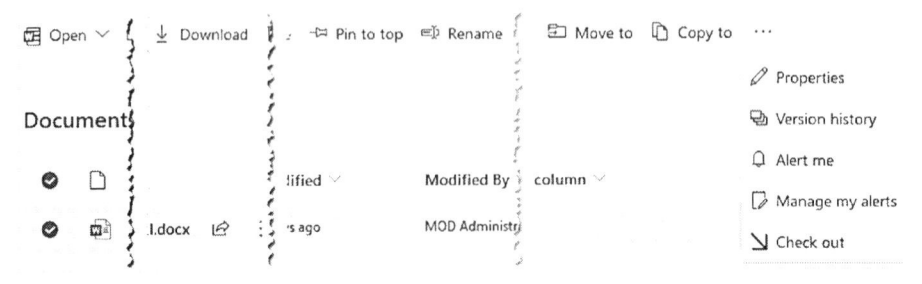

⊞ Open ⌄	↓ Download	⊷ Pin to top	✎ Rename	⬚ Move to	⎗ Copy to	⋯

Documents

                                                                                     ⌀ Properties
                                                                                      🕘 Version history
                                                                                      🔔 Alert me

    ⊘   ▢   !ified ⌄   Modified By   column ⌄
                                                                                      ✎ Manage my alerts
    ⊘   ▣   .docx ⎘   's ago   MOD Administr
                                                                                      ↘ Check out

- Open the file. Office files have two options: open in the desktop app or open in the browser. This button is not visible for all file types.
- Download the file to your computer.
- Pin a thumbnail of the file or folder above the list of items.

Documents

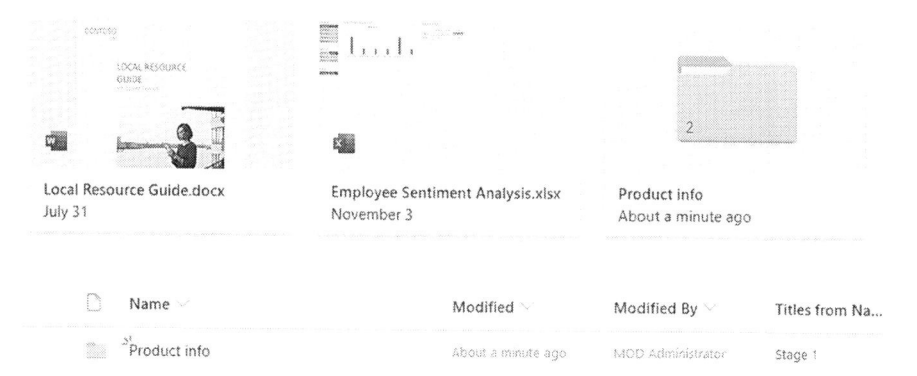

| Local Resource Guide.docx | Employee Sentiment Analysis.xlsx | Product info |
| July 31 | November 3 | About a minute ago |

| Name | Modified | Modified By | Titles from Na... |
| Product info | About a minute ago | MOD Administrator | Stage 1 |

When an item has been pinned, the command is changed into 'Edit pin' when the same item is selected again. Now you can unpin or change the position of the pin.

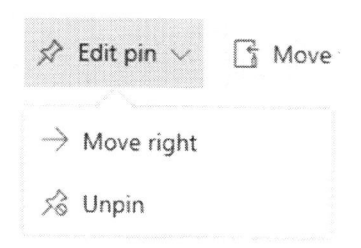

Edit pin   Move
→ Move right
   Unpin

- Rename, opens a dialog where you can give the file a new name.
- Move to, moves the item into or out of a subfolder in the current library, to another library that you have access to or to your OneDrive for Business.
- Copy to, copies the item to a subfolder in the current library, to another library that you have access to or to your OneDrive for Business.
- Properties, opens a right pane that shows the values in all columns and gives the option to edit them.
- Check out a file when you don't want other users to see your changes, or you don't want the changes to be visible in the version history yet.

5.2.3 Document Tile

When you hover the mouse cursor over the file name in a document library with the modern interface, a tile will be visible. It shows the share icon and a 'See details' link that opens the file's Information pane. Several file types also have views information.

When the file is an Office file, there is an 'Inside look' section with information about average reading time for the document and a part of the text.

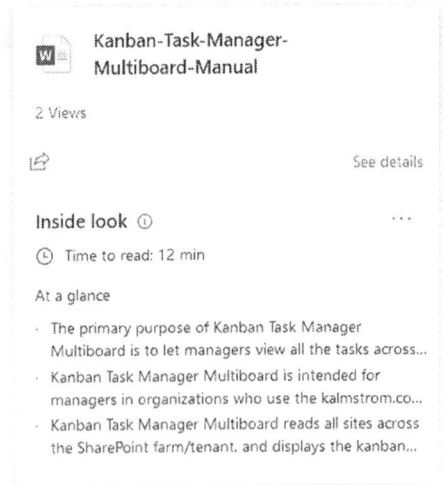

5.3 CREATE A LIBRARY APP

You can create a new library app from the "Your Apps" page, as described in chapter 3.

The 'New' button in a modern SharePoint homepage or Site contents also gives the option 'Document library'.

When you use this option to create a document library, you will not be directed to the "Your Apps" page.

Instead, a right pane will open, where you can enter a name and a description for the new library.

A document library created with the 'Document library' option from the homepage or Site contents, will open when you have filled out the details and clicked on 'Create'.

5.3.1 Auto-Created Columns

When you create a new document library app, several columns will be added automatically. You can see all of them in the Library settings.

The automatically created columns "Name", "Modified" and "Modified by" are visible in the default "All Documents" view.

The "Name" column is for the file name and should of course always be visible, but you can very well hide the other two columns from a view. They are filled out automatically.

The columns "Created", "Created by", "Title" and "Checked out to" are also created automatically, but they are not displayed in the "All Documents" view. "Created" and "Created by" are filled out automatically.

Only the "Name" and the "Title" columns are by default visible in the item form.

5.3.1.1 The Title Column and the Search Engine

The values in an app's "Title" column are important for the SharePoint search engine. The "Title" field has the highest rank of all, so the title is where SharePoint begins the search after you have written a search word or phrase.

Hits in the title also comes first in the results. For the search to work well, it is therefore important that "Title" columns are filled out with words that give relevant information. Unfortunately, the "Title" field is often left empty in library items.

When the "Title" column in a SharePoint library is empty, the file name becomes prominent. Imagine how the search will work if you and other users leave the "Title" field empty and don't change the default file name, 'Document', 'Book' or 'Presentation'!

As mentioned above, a "Title" column is created automatically when you create a new library app. It is however not visible in the default view, so to enter something there, you must edit the file properties.

When you create a new item in a *list* app, you cannot save it until the "Title" field is filled out, but when you create a new item in a SharePoint library, there is no such compulsion. On the contrary, the "Title" field is rather hidden.

Another reason that people sometimes avoid filling out "Title" fields, or fill them out badly, might be that they don't understand the meaning of the field.

Thus, I recommend that you add the "Title" column to the default view and change "Title" into something that is more explanatory. Renaming the "Title" column can also be an alternative to adding a new Single line of text column to the app.

5.4 ADD CONTENT TO DOCUMENT LIBRARIES

You can add content to a SharePoint document library either by creating a new Office document directly in SharePoint or by uploading an existing file to the library.

The upload of existing files can be done in several different ways, and I will describe them below. Another way, to synchronize SharePoint libraries with folders in the File Explorer, is described in section 7.4, Synchronize with a Local Folder.

5.4.1 Upload Files

All file types can be uploaded to SharePoint libraries. When you add files to SharePoint, they will be copied to items in the library. They will not be removed from your computer.

When you copy files to a SharePoint library the file name is always kept, but the file creator, creation and modified dates, security settings and most other metadata is not copied to SharePoint. Instead, the addition of such metadata will start from scratch after the upload.

5.4.1.1 Select Multiple Files

Use one of these methods to select multiple files in your File Explorer:

- To select any files, hold down the Ctrl key and click on the files you want to add.
- To select files that are sorted together, hold down the Shift key while you click on the first file and then on the last file. Now all files between the first and the last file will be selected.
- To select all files in a folder, hold down the Ctrl key and press the A key.

5.4.1.2 Upload Button

Click on the 'Upload' button in the command bar to upload one or several files to a SharePoint library.

Browse to the item(s) on your computer that you want to upload and click OK. Now the file(s) or folder(s) will be uploaded.

When you upload a file that has the same name as an existing file in the library, you will get a question about replacing the file.

Here, you can also upload a folder, and a file that should be used as a template, *refer to* 5.9.1, Upload Office Template.

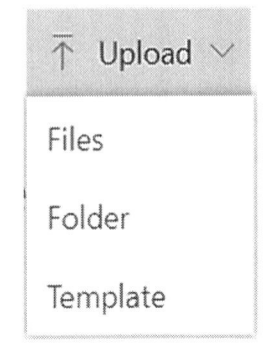

5.4.1.3 Drag and Drop

It is possible to drag and drop files from a computer to a SharePoint Online library. This can be done with one file or with multiple files at the same time, so drag and drop is a fast and convenient way to add files to libraries.

1. Open the File Explorer on your computer in a small window over the SharePoint library window or put the two windows side by side using the Windows button + the left and right keys.
2. Select the file(s) you want to copy to the library.

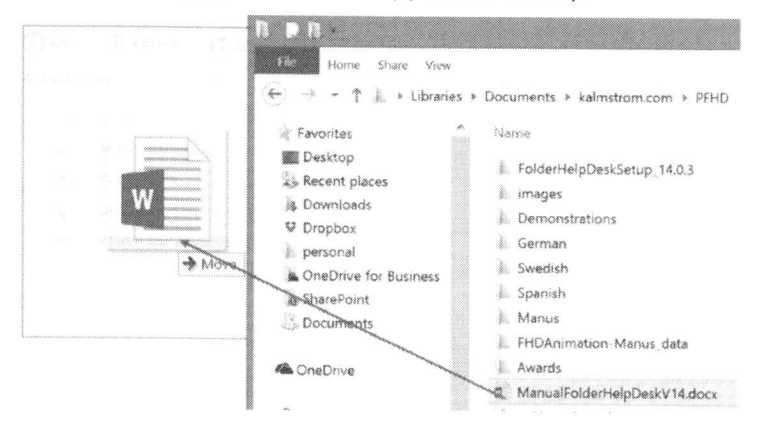

3. Drag the files to the box that becomes visible in the library and drop them there.

You may also drag the files to the browser icon. The browser will then open in the latest visited window, and if that is the SharePoint library you can drop the file as described in point 3 above.

5.4.1.4   Save a File to SharePoint

These are the steps to save an open Office file from a computer to a SharePoint document library.

1. Open an Excel, PowerPoint or Word file.
2. Open the 'Files' tab.
3. Select 'Save as'.
4. Click on the 'Sites' button.

   A choice of sites that you have access to will open.
5. Select a site.
6. Select a library.

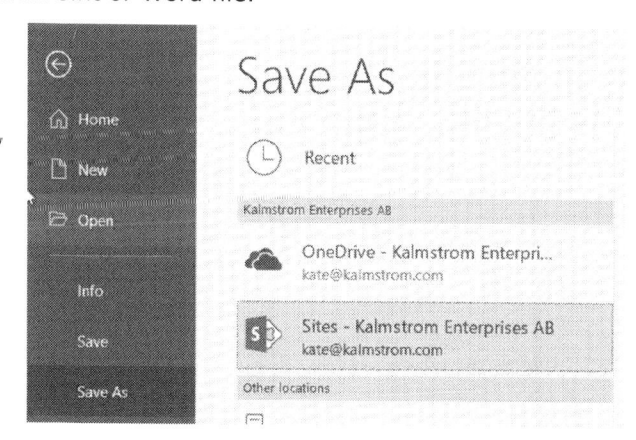

5.4.2 Rename a File

If you want to rename any file type in a document library, you can change the name in already saved or uploaded files in several ways:

- Switch the library to Grid view mode. Select the cell that has the name of the new file and change the name.
- Select the item and click on 'Rename' in the command bar or under the ellipsis. Now a dialog will open where you can change the name of the file.

- Click on 'Properties' in the command bar, or open the Information pane and click on 'Edit all' to change the file name and any other properties.

5.4.3   Create an Office File in a Library

A good way to get content into a SharePoint document library, is to create a new file from the library. Click on the '+ New' button in the command bar to start the creation.

By default, you will now have a choice of creating an Office file or a folder. When you select one of the files, a blank template will open.

You can also add a link as an item in the library, edit the '+New' menu and add a custom template. There might also be a survey option in the dropdown.

It is however quite possible that you encounter a document library that gives only one, or a few, options. The '+New' menu can be edited, and document libraries may have a custom content type that restricts the file type options when you create a new document. There might also be more options than the default ones.

Follow these steps to create a new file in a SharePoint library:

+ New ∨   ↑ Upload ∨

- Folder
- Word document
- Excel workbook
- PowerPoint presentation
- OneNote notebook
- Link
- Edit New menu
- + Add template

1. Open the library where you want to create the new file and click on the '+New' button.
2. Click on one of the template options.
3. Click 'Yes' to the warning message.

> **Microsoft Word**   ×
> ⚠ The document you are trying to open is a template. Would you like to open and edit as a standard document?
> [Yes]   [No]

4. A new document will open, by default in the online version of the document type you selected and in a new tab.
5. Now you can start working with the document. Changes are saved automatically.

To work in the desktop version instead, click on 'Open in …' on top of the ribbon. In Word, this command is found under the 'Editing' button instead.

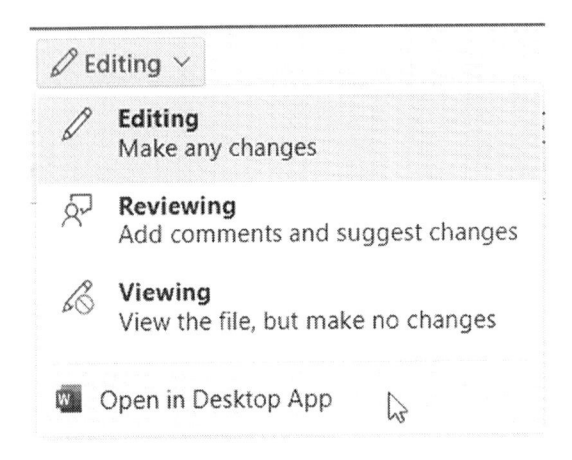

5.4.3.1 Naming

When new files are created inside a SharePoint library, they get a default name: Document, Book or Presentation, depending on file type.

If you don't change the default name, the library will eventually contain many documents with different content but with the same, non-descriptive names. That will of course make it difficult to find the correct file on each occasion.

Before you return to the library, you should therefore give the new file a good name that explains what the document contains.

- For a Word or PowerPoint file, click on the default name, 'Document' or 'Presentation' above the ribbon. Now you can give the file a new name, and there are links to the site, to the document library and to the Version history (which of course only is interesting for old files, not for new ones).

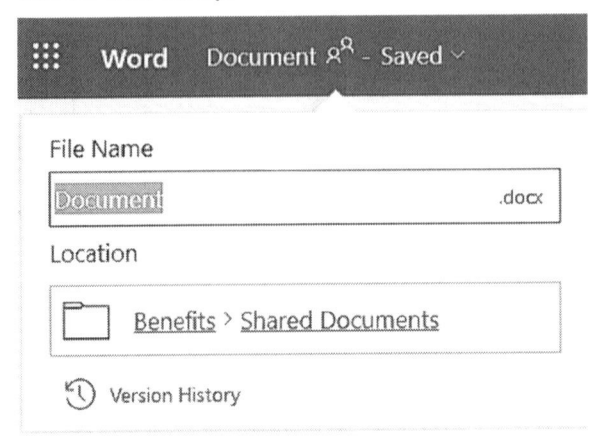

- When this is written, Excel files don't have the same possibility for name giving. Instead of the document name, there are links to the site and the library to the right above the ribbon. The default name is in the middle, and you can just click in it and type or paste the new name.

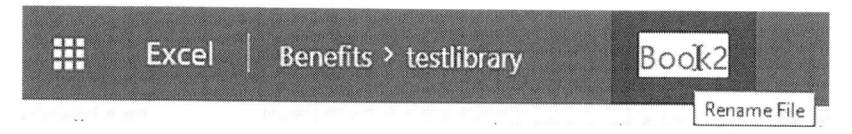

5.5 FIND A FILE LINK

When you have the link to a file in a library, you can use it to share the file or embed it in a page. You can of course open the file and take the URL from the browser's address bar, but with the 'Copy link' command under the item ellipsis or in the command bar, you will have a possibility to set permissions on the file before you share it.

Refer to 9.4, Share a File, for more information on file sharing and permissions.

5.6 EDIT A FILE OR AN ITEM

When you select an item in a library app Standard view mode, you either want to edit the file or the metadata.

5.6.1 Edit Properties

In the Grid view mode, you can edit the metadata of all items by simply changing the values in the cells.

In the Standard view mode, click on 'Properties' in the command bar, or open the Information pane and click on 'Edit all' to change the properties, as described in the Rename section above.

5.6.2 Edit an Office File

When you want to edit an Office file, you can just click on the file name to open the file in edit mode. By default, it will open in the browser edition.

If you use the 'Open' button in the command bar, you will have a choice where to open the file.

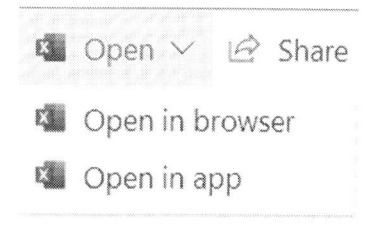

The Online editions of the Office apps run in the browser, and they automatically save your files to the document library where they were created or opened. These online editions are similar to the desktop/client editions, but some features are missing.

On the other hand, an online document can be edited by multiple people at the same time, which in some scenarios is a fantastic benefit, and the browser editions have some features that facilitates cooperation: different kinds of editing and a possibility to have a Comments thread in a right pane.

The PowerPoint browser edition also has options for presenting the slideshow.

5.6.2.1   Editing by Multiple Users

Several people can work on the same Word Online, Excel Online or PowerPoint Online file at the same time in a SharePoint Online library, where all participants have access to the file. You can also use a shared OneDrive for Business folder, *refer to* 7.3, Sharing from OneDrive.

If you select to edit a Word, Excel or PowerPoint file in the Online edition, and another person is editing the same document, you will have a message about it:

   Antonio Moreno is editing this document.

You can also see where in the document the other user is working.

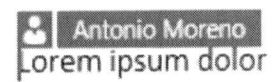

Antonio Moreno
Lorem ipsum dolor

You may continue with your editing, because all changes, no matter which one of the users who made them, will be visible in the document.

You can be more than two users on the same document. I have seen around 15 people collaborating on a document in Word Online!

5.7   CHECK OUT / CHECK IN

When you work with an Office file that is stored in a SharePoint document library and don't want other users to see your changes, or you don't want them to be visible in the version history quite yet, you can check out the file.

A check out also prevents that several people edit the same file simultaneously. When a file is checked out, you can edit it online or offline and save it as many times as you wish. No other user will be able to see your changes until you check in the file again.

When a file is checked out, it has a red icon to the right of the file name.

5.7.1 Check Out / Check In Commands

There is a 'Check out' option under the ellipsis at the file name and under the ellipsis in the command bar when a file is selected.

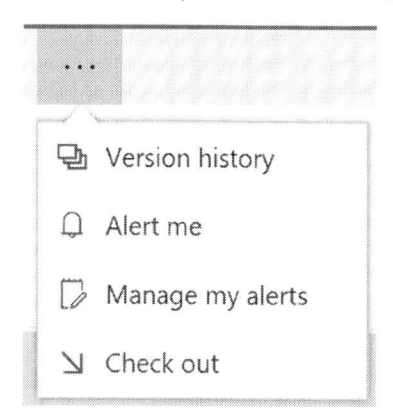

When you have checked out a file, the 'Check out' command is replaced with two other commands: 'Check in' and 'Discard check out'.

Check in the file when you want other users to see your changes.

Discard the check out if you don't want to keep your changes. When you do that, the Version history of the file will not be affected.

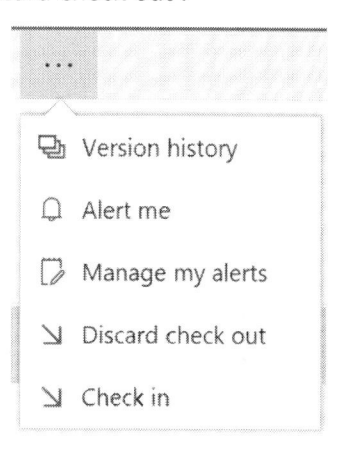

5.7.2 Require Check Out

When you create a document library, you can decide that Check out should be mandatory. This is set in the Library settings >Versioning settings. The default setting is No.

If you set check out to be required before editing in a library, you will overcome the issue with several people unintentionally editing the same document. On the other hand, you will probably have issues because people forget to check in the edited file again!

5.8 Copy Items

With the 'Copy to' link in the command bar and under the item ellipsis, you can copy one or more items from one document library in the tenant to another. Select first site and then library (and folder) to copy to.

1. Select one or multiple items.
2. Click on 'Copy to' in the command bar and under the item ellipsis.
3. Select a site to copy to.
4. Select a library (and folder) to copy to.

The item in the destination document library will always contain the file, but metadata is only added to the new library when there are columns for it in the destination library.

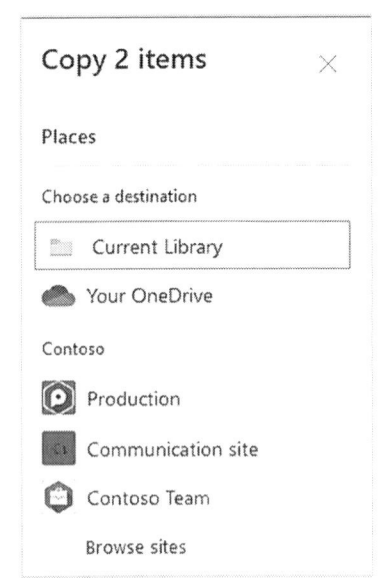

When the source library and the destination library have columns of the same type with the same name, the copied item's values in these fields will be copied too.

5.9 '+New' Menu Options

The '+New' dropdown in SharePoint libraries has two options that cannot be used with the classic interface: Edit new menu and Add template.

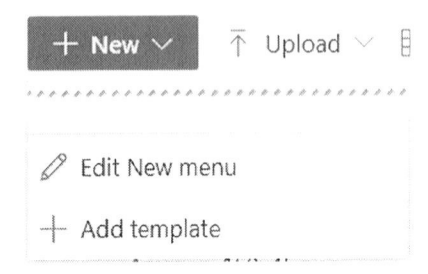

5.9.1 Upload Office Template

In the modern library interface, you can upload any Office document and use it as a template. Create the template in your desktop application and save it with a suitable name. You don't have to use a specific template format, .docx. .pptx and .xlsx will do fine.

1. Click on the '+New' button in the command bar and select '+ Add template', OR Click on the 'Upload' button and select 'Template'.

2. Select the template you have created. It will now be uploaded and added to the templates in the '+New' dropdown.

Note that the template you uploaded will not be displayed to other library users if they switch to the classic interface.

5.9.2 Edit the '+New' Menu

When you want users to only use custom templates when they create new documents in a modern SharePoint library, or when you want to limit their choices, you can edit the menu to only show the template(s) that should be used.

The image to the right shows an example.

1. Click on the '+New' button and select 'Edit New menu'.
2. A right pane with all templates will open, and you can uncheck the templates you want to hide.
3. To reorder the templates, select any template in the right pane, open its ellipsis and move it up or down.

   You can also just drag the templates to your preferred order.
4. Save your changes.

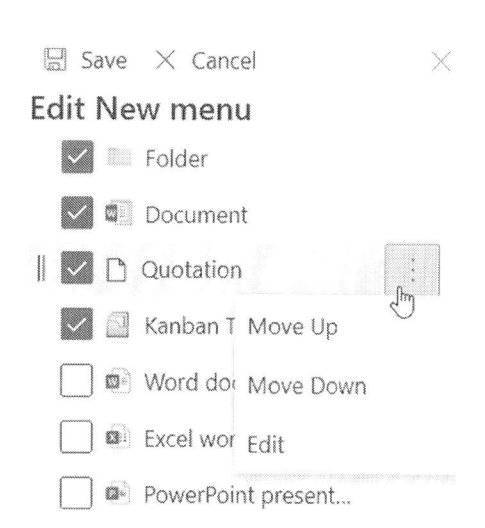

Now the modern interface will only show the options you have selected, but, but your settings will not reflect to the classic interface.

5.10 SUMMARY

This chapter about SharePoint libraries has shown how to create content in libraries and how to upload files and templates. I have also explained how you can check out documents to keep your changes to yourself and how several people can work with the same Excel, PowerPoint or Word Online file.

A discussion about the "Title" field in library items has also been included in this chapter, and in addition to that, I have described how to edit, copy and move files and properties and how to edit the '+New' menu.

In the next chapter, I will introduce SharePoint sites.

6 SHAREPOINT SITES

The sites are the core of SharePoint. All content is added, and all work is done, within the context of a site. Therefore, each site has a huge number of settings that control how the site works and looks.

SharePoint sites can be customized in many ways. You can, and should, add pages and different kinds of apps to the site. These pages and apps can be customized, so how a SharePoint site looks and how it is used is very flexible.

By default, everyone who has an account in the tenant has permission to create a site. Therefore, I will start this chapter with clarifying a few terms and introducing some site features.

After that, I will describe what kind of sites you can create and explain how you create and manage them.

6.1 SITE TERMS

Before we go deeper into the sites, there are some terms that you need to understand.

6.1.1 Homepage

Each site has its own URL, and by default sites that users can create have the URL https://[tenant name].sharepoint.com/sites/[site name].

https://m365x446726.sharepoint.com/sites/ContosoNews

When you add content to the site, the name and storage place of that content will be added to the site URL.

When you enter the URL in a web browser, or click on a link with the site URL, you will reach the site's homepage. From that homepage, you can then reach all other contents in the site.

6.1.2 Home Site

The homepage in the Home site is the top SharePoint landing page for your organization's tenant. It usually has links to all important information, and news that concerns the whole organization should be published here.

The URL of the Home site is the tenant domain + .sharepoint.com (for example https://kalmstromnet.sharepoint.com).

The Home site is created automatically when the 365 tenant is set up.

6.1.3 Site and Site Collection

In SharePoint settings, you can find the term "site collection" instead of site. To understand this book, you can just translate "site collection" into "site".

6.2 SITE TYPES

SharePoint has several types of sites, but only four of them are commonly used:

- The modern Communication site
- The modern Group Team site
- The modern Team site without a group
- The classic Team site

Even if three of the site types are modern and one is classic, the three Team site types have common features that are not present in the Communication site. On the other hand, the Communication site has some features that are not present in any of the other site types.

Team sites and Communication sites also look different. SharePoint Team sites have the Site navigation to the left on the page. Communication sites instead have the Site navigation on top of the page.

In this chapter, I will only go into the two first site types, because they can by default be created by all users. Users without access to the SharePoint Admin center can only create the Team site without a group and the classic Team site if they are allowed to create subsites, *refer to* 6.8, Subsites.

You might encounter these site types in your tenant, and if you understand the Communication and Group Team sites, I don't think you will have any problems to figure out how the other site types work.

6.2.1 Group Team Site

The Group Team site is probably the site type that you will work most with, as it is intended for collaboration within a team.

By default, the homepage of the Group Team site has web parts for News, Activity, Quick links and Documents. This page is a site page, so it can be customized and have other web parts. You will learn how to do that in chapter 8.

Above the web parts, there is a command bar. Here, site members with edit permissions will see a "New" button that allows them to add content to the site.

The command bar also has a button for Site details. It opens a right pane with a site description and version history information. The buttons in the right part of the command bar are used when the homepage is customized.

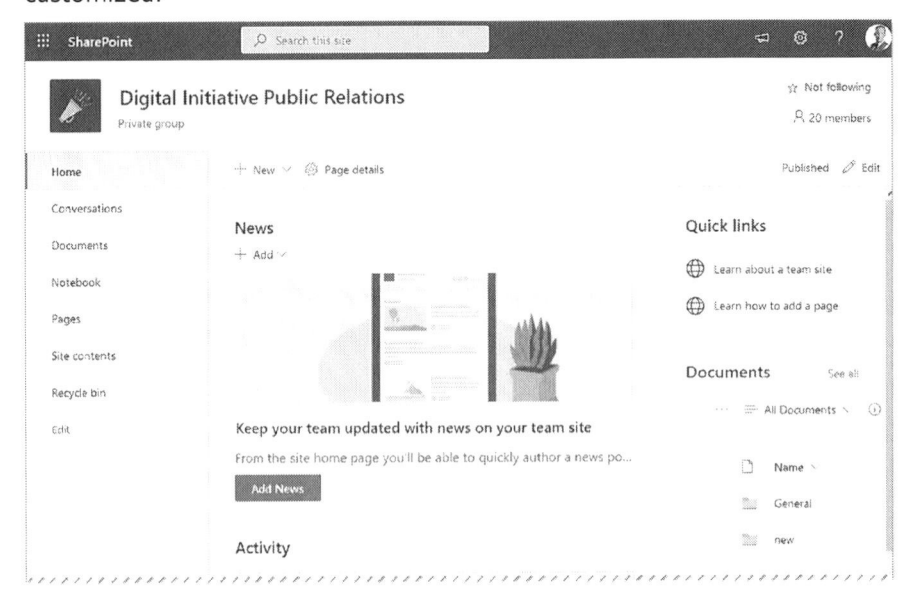

6.2.1.1   Microsoft 365 Group

The Group Team site is connected to a Microsoft 365 group, that will be created automatically together with the site.

A Microsoft 365 group is a group of colleagues that share resources, so in addition to the Group Team site, the Microsoft 365 group has other shared apps and services. There is always a shared e-mail inbox, and the group e-mail name is by default the same as the Group Team site name.

You can reach the Group's inbox, settings and other shared resources from the 'Conversations' link in the Group Team site's Site navigation.

6.2.1.2 Microsoft Teams

Microsoft 365 groups often cooperate via Microsoft Teams. When the group is not connected to Teams, a team can easily be created via a prompt below the Site navigation in the Group Team site.

When the group has been connected to Teams, a link to Teams will be added in the Site navigation in the Group Team site.

When the Microsoft 365 group is connected to both a SharePoint Group Team site and Microsoft Teams, the group can also be managed in Teams.

> **Microsoft Teams**
> Communicate with your colleagues in real time by creating a Team for your Office 365 Group.
> Create a Team

The apps and pages in the Group Team site can easily be added to Teams, so that people work with the SharePoint content in Teams instead of going to the SharePoint site.

Refer to my book *Microsoft Teams from Scratch* for more information about Teams.

6.2.2 Communication Site

Just as the name suggests, a Communication site is used to communicate information, not for collaboration in the first place. Usually, a Communication site has only a few authors but a larger number of readers.

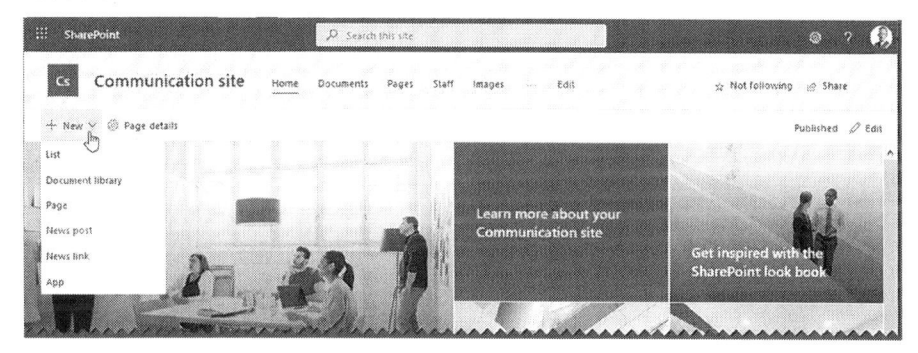

[Screenshot of a SharePoint Communication site showing the homepage with navigation tabs (Home, Documents, Pages, Staff, Images, Edit), a New menu expanded showing List, Document library, Page, News post, News link, App options, and banner sections "Learn more about your Communication site" and "Get inspired with the SharePoint look book"]

The Communication site has the Site navigation on top of the page, not to the left as other site types.

Below the Site navigation, the homepage of the Communication site has the same kind of command bar as the Group Team site.

6.2.2.1 Templates

When you create a new Communication site, you can select one of the homepage templates:

89

- Topic – this is the template that is used for the default Home site Communication site, *refer to* 6.1.2, Home Site. Use the Topic template when you want to share information about events, news and similar content.
- Showcase – a template that makes it easy to show photos and images.

These templates come with a set of web parts that are especially suitable for information sharing, so that you only need to modify them to get a good-looking homepage.

You can also choose to have a blank homepage and add the web parts you want to use to it.

6.3 CREATE A SITE

By default, all users can create Communication and Group Team sites from the SharePoint Online start page, *refer to* 2.1.2. You can also create Group Team sites from OneDrive for Business, *refer to* chapter 7.

When you have created a site, you will be its owner, and by default also its Site admin. SharePoint administrators can apply another Site admin, and in that case, there are some limitations to what you can do with the site. In any case, it is the Site owner who owns all content in the site.

When you have created a site, it will appear among your followed sites on the SharePoint Online start page.

Here, I will describe the site creation from the SharePoint Online start page. The first creation steps are the same for the two site types.

1. Click on the 'Create site' button in the top left corner of the SharePoint Online start page.
2. Select the site type you want to use.

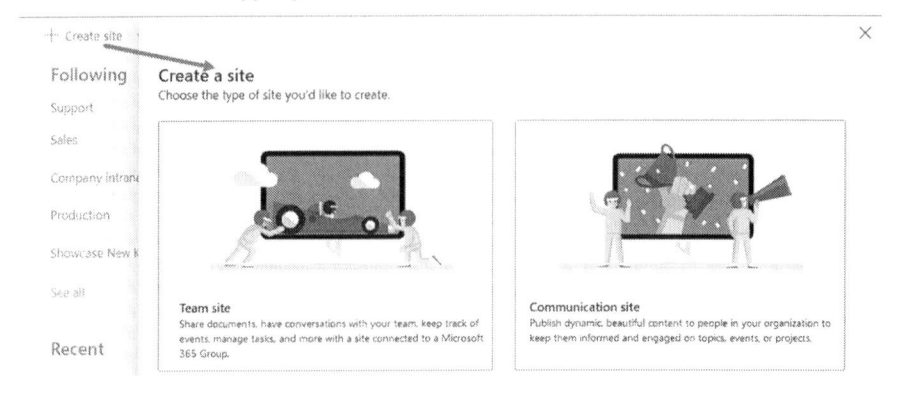

6.3.1 Team Site

When you select the 'Team site' option, you are creating a Microsoft 365 group and some group resources at the same time. You will not only be the Site owner and Site admin but also the Group owner.

Fill out the site name and description. The group's e-mail address and the site address will be added automatically when you have entered the site name. Any spaces in the name will be removed.

By default, the Group Team site is private, and if you keep that setting you must add the group members manually.

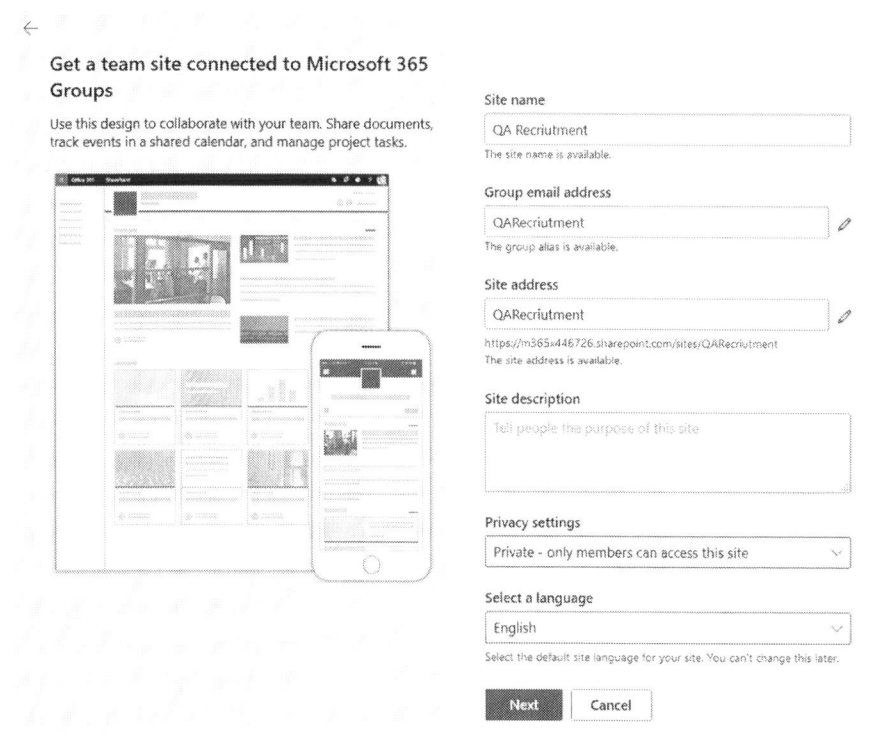

When you select the other option, public, all users in the tenant will have access to the new Group Team site. This is not recommended, unless the organization is very small.

Click on 'Next' to add group members. You can also add additional owners, and it is often good to have at least one more owner.

Start typing, and select the colleagues you want to add from the suggestions you get.

Add group members

Group members will receive an email welcoming them to the new site and Microsoft 365 Group

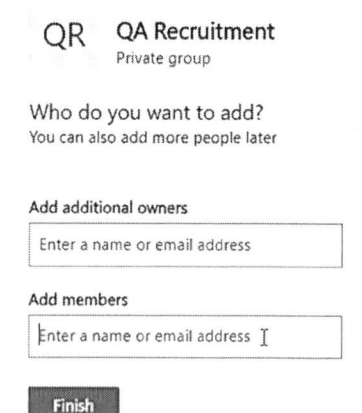

QR **QA Recruitment**
Private group

Who do you want to add?
You can also add more people later

Add additional owners

[Enter a name or email address]

Add members

[Enter a name or email address]

Finish

When you click on 'Finish', the site and the Microsoft 365 group will be created. The site will open automatically, and all members will receive an e-mail where they are welcomed to the site.

6.3.2 Communication site

When you select to create a Communication site, you must first select one of the templates.

← Back

Communication Site

Choose a design

| Topic | ∨ |

- Topic
- Showcase
- Blank

Then you only need to give the site a name and a description and click on 'Finish' to create the new site.

When you have created a Communication site, nobody but you have access to it. You need to invite people to the site, and in chapter 8 I will explain how that is done.

6.4 SITE CONTENTS

To see all the contents of a site, click on the 'Site contents' link in the Site navigation, or open the 365 Settings icon and select 'Site contents'.

A page with links to all content in the site will open. It also has links to the site's statistics, workflows, settings and recycle bin above the actual contents of the site.

📈 Site usage   ⟲ Site workflows   ⚙ Site settings   🗑 Recycle bin (7)

The modern Site contents interface looks like the document library interface, but it has two tabs: one for subsites and one for other content.

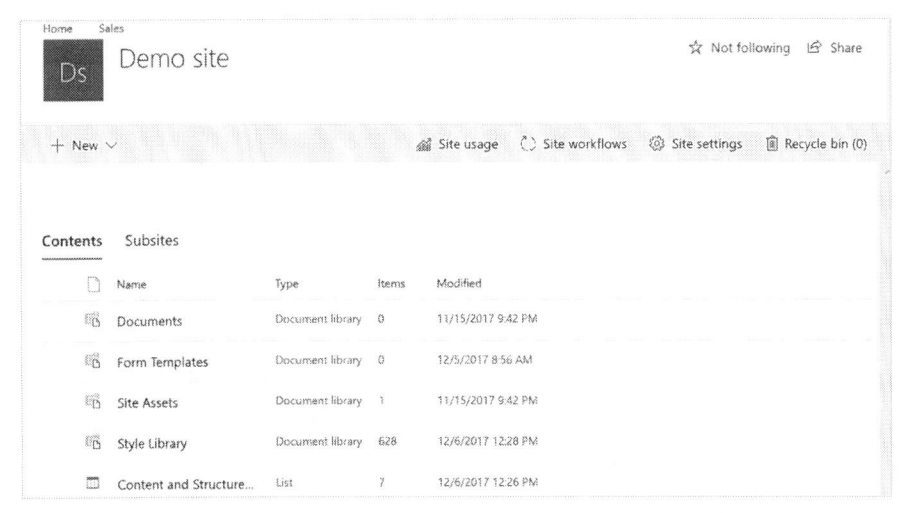

Demo site screenshot showing Contents tab with Documents, Form Templates, Site Assets, Style Library, and Content and Structure items.

the right of each app name in the Site contents, an ellipsis becomes visible when you hover the mouse over the item. Click on the ellipsis to reach more information about the app.

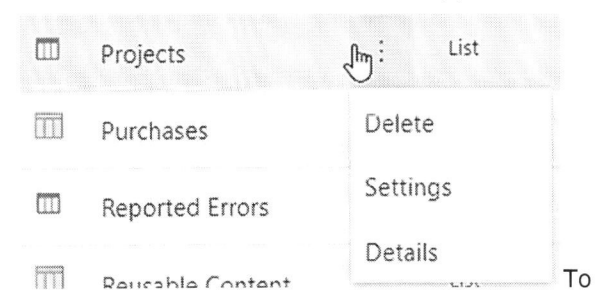

Screenshot showing ellipsis menu with Delete, Settings, Details options for Projects list.

Under the Contents tab, the app ellipses let you delete the app, reach the app settings and see details.

93

When you select the 'Details' option under the ellipsis, you will have a description of the app. You can also create another app of the same type by clicking on the ADD IT button.

Document Library

DESCRIPTION
Use a document library to store, organize, sync, and share documents with people. You can use co-authoring, versioning, and check out to work on documents together. With your documents in one place, everybody can get the latest versions whenever they need them. You can also sync your documents to your local computer for offline access.

ADD IT

Under the Subsites tab, the ellipsis gives a link to the Site contents of the subsite. The subsite Site contents is built in the same way as the Site contents of the root site.

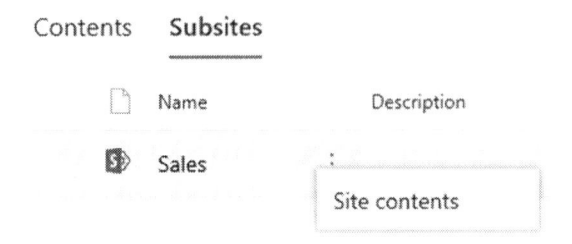

Contents **Subsites**

Name	Description
Sales	

Site contents

In the Site contents command bar, there is a 'New' button to create new apps, pages and subsites. You already know how to create apps here, and we will have a look at the pages in chapter 8.

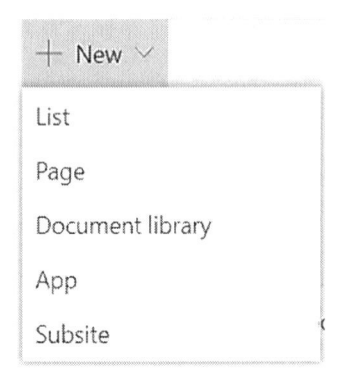

+ New ∨
- List
- Page
- Document library
- App
- Subsite

6.5 SITE SETTINGS

The administration of a site is most often done in the Site settings. You can reach the settings for the current site via the settings button in the Site contents, *see* above, and from the 365 Settings icon.

When you use the 365 Settings icon, you will first see a 'Site information' in the dropdown. That command takes you to a right pane where you can upload a site icon, give a description, delete the site and more.

Click on 'View all site settings' to reach the full site settings page.

When you use the 'Site settings' button in the Site contents, you will reach the full Site settings page directly.

The Site settings page has links to site control pages, grouped under headings to be easier to find. Which controls you can find depend on the site type and on what permissions you have.

I will inform about some features in the Site settings later in this book.

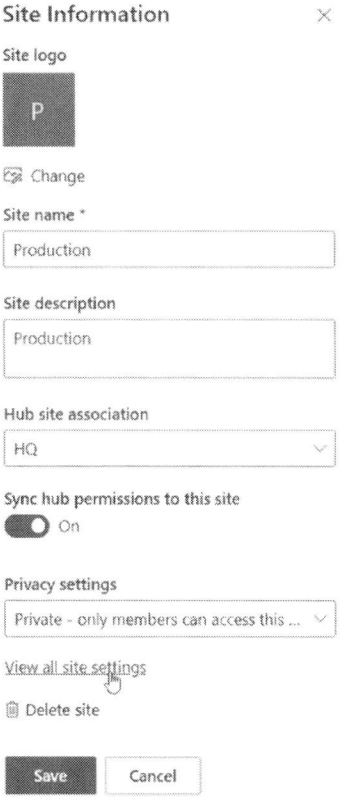

6.6 Change the Look

Under the 365 Settings icon, you can find a link called 'Change the look'. It opens a right pane where you can select a theme and customize the site's header with an image, background color and more.

Communication sites also have choices for the navigation and the footer.

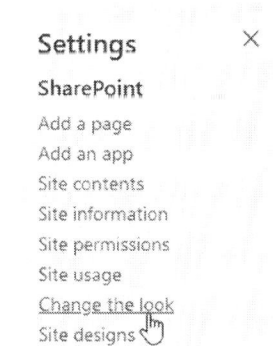

6.7 HUB FAMILIES

SharePoint sites have no connection with each other. Each site is a separate unit with its own permissions and management. You can link to other sites but that is all – unless you register a hub site and create a hub family.

A hub family consists of one hub site and several other sites that are associated with the hub site. The Communication site type is often used as hub site.

Within a hub family, related sites can be connected based on project, department, division, region or anything else. It is easy for users to discover related content, news and site activity across all associated sites.

When you associate a site with a hub site, this will happen to the associated site:

- Content like news and activity from your site will be visible on the hub site homepage.
- You can no longer edit the theme of your site, as it will use the hub site theme.
- Your site will inherit the specific Hub navigation from the hub site.
- You can choose to sync site permissions with hub permissions to increase site access for viewers.
- Content from this and other associated sites will be prioritized in searches from the hub site.

Only Global and SharePoint admins can register a site as a hub site, but all site owners can associate their sites with hub sites. A site can only be associated with one hub site.

When a site has been registered as a hub site, it gets a new navigation bar on top, below the 365 navigation bar. Here, the hub site owner should add links to all the associated sites. As the associated sites inherit the Hub navigation, all sites in the family can then be reached from all the included sites.

The Hub navigation can be displayed cascading – in a row – or as a mega menu, *see* the image above.

6.7.1 Associate with a Hub Site

By default, all site owners can associate their sites with a hub site, but this permission can be restricted in the SharePoint Admin center to only allow specific people.

To associate a site with a hub site from inside the site, open the 365 Settings icon and select 'Site information'. There, you can select a hub site from a dropdown, *see* the image at 6.7, Site Settings, above

When you have selected the hub site and clicked on 'Save', the site will be associated either immediately or after approval from the hub site owner.

When you see the hub site navigation bar in the top right corner of the site, your will know that the site has been (approved and) associated.

Note that the associated site will inherit theme of the hub site, so you cannot edit the look of your site once you've associated it with a hub site.

6.7.2 Hub Permissions

In a hub family, each associated site has its own permissions, just as the hub site has. Hub site owners can however give visitor permission to people and groups, and these permissions can be synchronized to the associated sites.

When 'Sync hub permissions' has been turned on in the hub site, the associated sites will have a 'Hub' tab with permission information under the 365 Settings icon > Site permissions.

Here, site owners can set the synchronization to On and see information about the people and groups that have access to the hub.

In the image to the right, three Group Team sites have been associated to the HQ hub site. As the three Group Team sites are used by one Microsoft 365 group each, these groups are displayed as hub visitors.

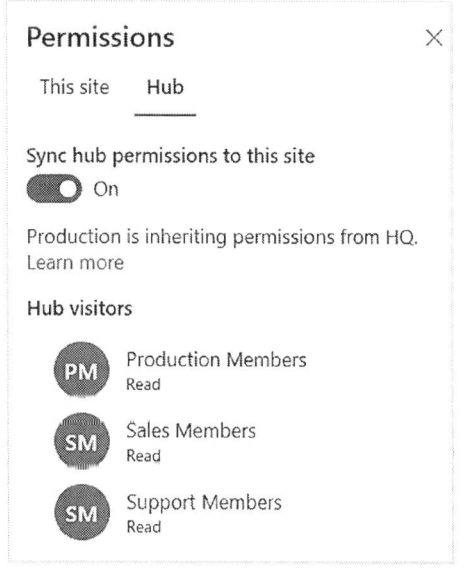

Permissions ×

This site   **Hub**

Sync hub permissions to this site
🔵 On

Production is inheriting permissions from HQ. Learn more

Hub visitors

(PM) Production Members
     Read

(SM) Sales Members
     Read

(SM) Support Members
     Read

The synchronization can be turned off anytime, and you should not sync the hub permissions if your site contains sensitive information.

6.8 SUBSITES

The hub family is one way of linking sites together. Another way is to create subsites and use shared navigation for all sites in the collection.

The subsite method to link sites creates a hierarchy, and that gives some drawbacks:

- Subsite URLs reflect that they are subsites to another site, so if you reorganize relationships you will break the links.
- Some features, like policies, apply to the root site and all subsites in a collection, whether you want it or not.
- By default, permissions are inherited between sites and subsites.

To create a new SharePoint subsite, open the Site contents of an existing site and click on 'New'. If you see a 'Subsite' link in the dropdown, you can create subsites.

When you create a new subsite, there are different kinds of site templates to select from. The default option is a modern Team site without a group, but you can also create a classic Team site.

Communication sites and Group Team sites cannot be created as subsites.

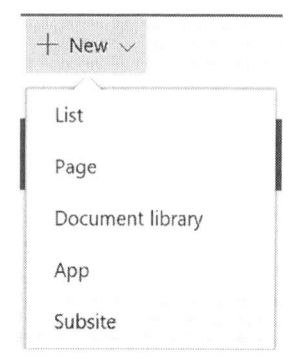

6.9 NAVIGATION

The navigation in a site can be edited in several ways, and I recommend that you consider which navigation options are the best for each site. Bad or lacking navigation can be very frustrating to users, while good navigation will make work smoother and more efficient.

6.9.1 Edit the Navigation

When you use the modern interface, the navigation can be easily edited via the 'Edit' link. You can find this link at the bottom of the Site navigation in Group Team sites and to the right in the Site navigation in Communication sites.

The 'Edit' command opens a left pane where you can see the Site navigation in edit mode.

::: SharePoint

Demos   Home   Sales   Development   Edit

Ds Demo site

Home

Sales

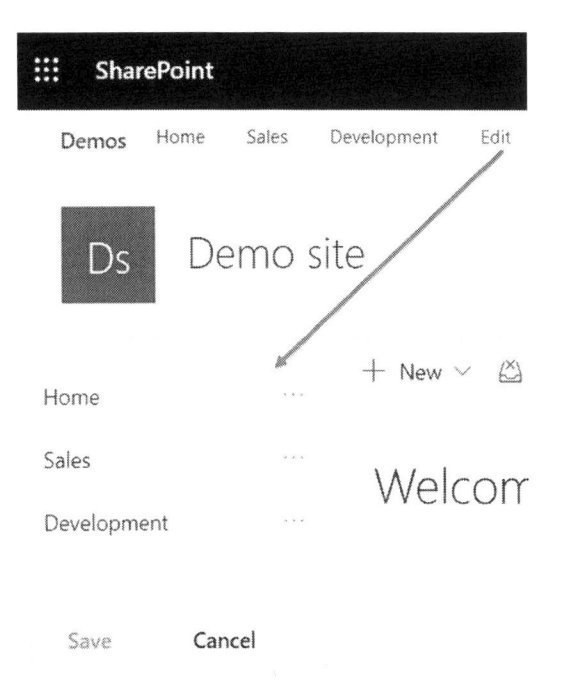

Development

+ New

Welcom

Save   Cancel

When the navigation is in edit mode, each link will have an ellipsis with various options, *see* the image below.

To add a new link, move the cursor to where you want to place the link and click on the plus sign that appears when it is possible to insert a new link (above 'Documents' in the image below).

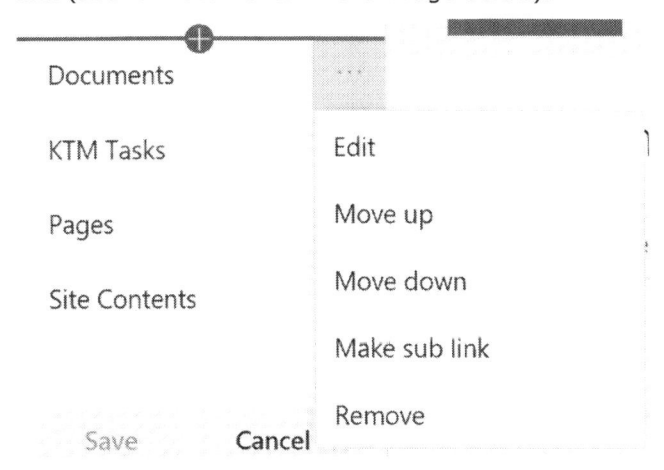

Documents

KTM Tasks

Pages

Site Contents

Edit

Move up

Move down

Make sub link

Remove

Save   Cancel

When you add a new link, the Hub navigation and Site navigation in Communication sites give an extra option: a choice between Link and Label. When Label is selected, the Address field is greyed out.

99

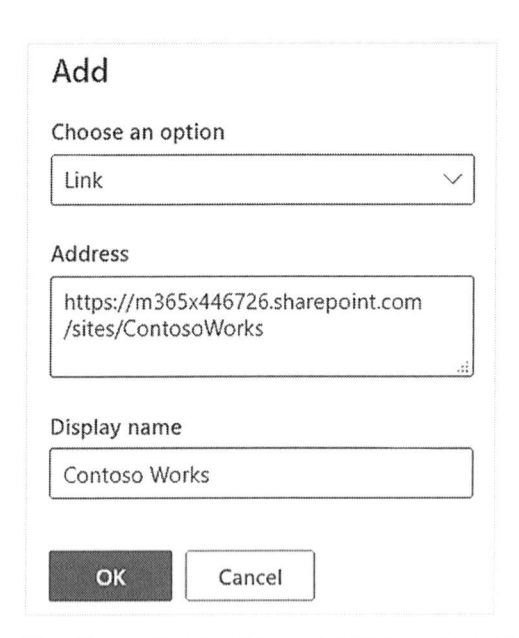

[Screenshot: Add dialog with Choose an option dropdown set to "Link", Address field containing "https://m365x446726.sharepoint.com/sites/ContosoWorks", Display name field containing "Contoso Works", and OK/Cancel buttons]

The Group Team site navigation pane instead have suggestions on links to shared group resources above the 'Address' and 'Display name' fields.

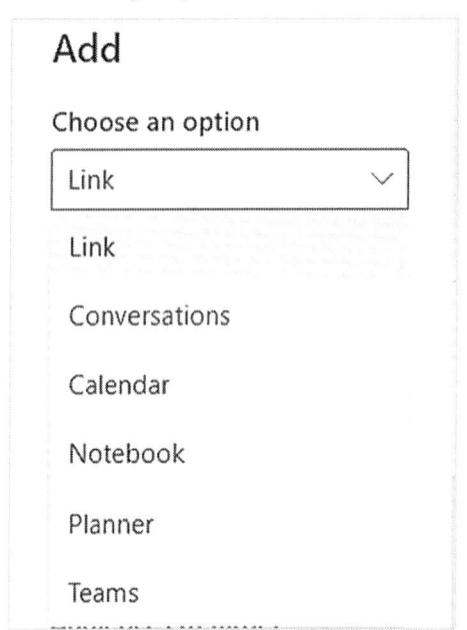

[Screenshot: Add dialog showing Choose an option dropdown expanded with options: Link, Conversations, Calendar, Notebook, Planner, Teams]

When you select one of the resources instead of the Link option, the link and the display name will be added automatically. Conversations give a link to the group's shared e-mail inbox.

100

6.9.2 Site Navigation Hierarchy

When you have many navigation links, it is useful to arrange them in groups with headings and sub links.

In all sites, you can arrange the links in a hierarchy by using the 'Make sub link' command in the Site navigation.

This command moves the selected link a little bit to the right. When you click on the command, it changes into 'Promote sub link' – which moves the link back again.

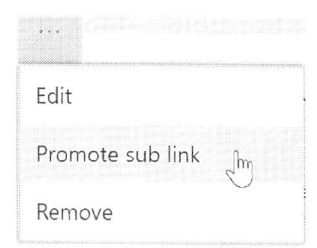

By combining links and sub links with labels, *see* above, you can even create a three level mega menu.

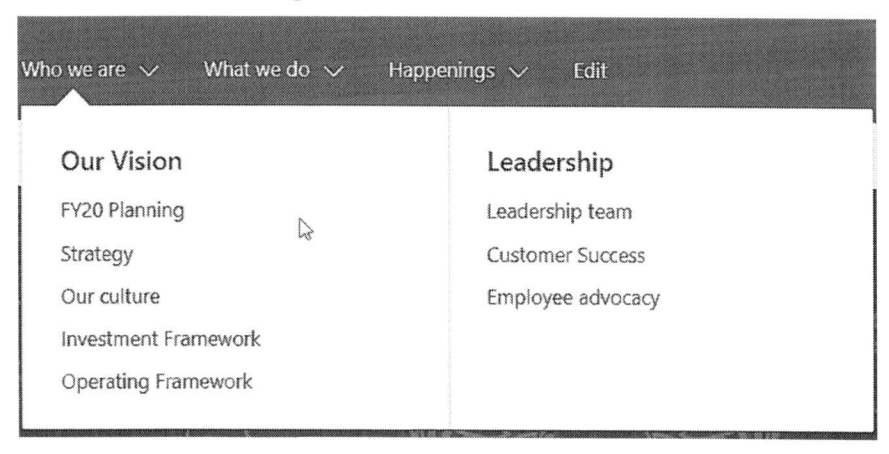

6.10 DELETE AND RESTORE A SITE

To delete a site that you have created, click on the 365 Settings icon and then on 'Site information'. Now you can delete the site and all its content directly from the right pane.

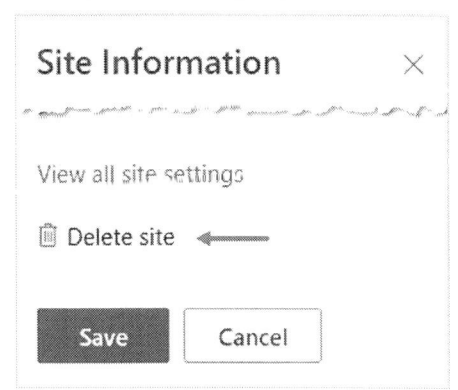

Deleted sites are kept for 93 days, but shared resources for a Microsoft 365 group are only kept for 30 days.

If you change your mind and want the site back again, you need to ask a SharePoint administrator to assist you, because sites can only be restored from the SharePoint Admin center.

6.11 Summary

In this chapter, you have learned about the main building block of SharePoint: the site. Now you should know what is common for all sites and what is the main difference between the Communication and Group Team site types. You understand how to create these sites, and you can manage them and connect them in a hub family.

SharePoint has several kinds of groups, and in this chapter, we have met the Microsoft 365 group. This is a group that share resources, among them a SharePoint Group Team site. You will encounter another kind of group chapter 9, Permissions and Sharing. In that chapter, you will also learn how to invite other people to a site that you have created.

In the next chapter, you will learn about each user's personal SharePoint site, OneDrive for Business.

7 ONEDRIVE FOR BUSINESS

OneDrive for Business contains a personal site that gives each SharePoint Online user a storage space of at least 1 TB. The files stored in that site are private, unless the owner decides to share them.

In this chapter, I will describe the OneDrive for Business document library and explain how you can share files from that library. I will also show how you can use OneDrive for Business to synchronize the OneDrive for Business library and any other SharePoint library that you have access to, with your computer.

Finally, I will explain how you can create a site that has many more of the useful SharePoint features than the default OneDrive for Business site.

The path to the OneDrive site collection looks like this:

https://TENANTNAME-my.sharepoint.com/personal/LOGINNAME/

(There is also a "OneDrive" included in Windows 8.1 and 10. It is connected to a Microsoft account – not to an organizational 365 account. It has less storage space and does not build on SharePoint, and that "OneDrive" is *not* what we are talking about here.)

7.1 THE "MY FILES" LIBRARY

When you click on the OneDrive for Business icon under the 365 App Launcher or at office.com, you will reach your OneDrive for Business document library, "My files".

As you see from the image below, the 'My files" library resembles other SharePoint document libraries, but some of the features you can find in other document libraries are missing.

You can share files and folders from the "My files" library, and you can add new content to it in the same way as with all SharePoint libraries. But the "My files" library lacks many of the other library features.

For example, you cannot create more columns for metadata or edit the existing columns, and there is no possibility to create different views.

Moreover, you cannot create new apps, pages or subsites from the "My files" library.

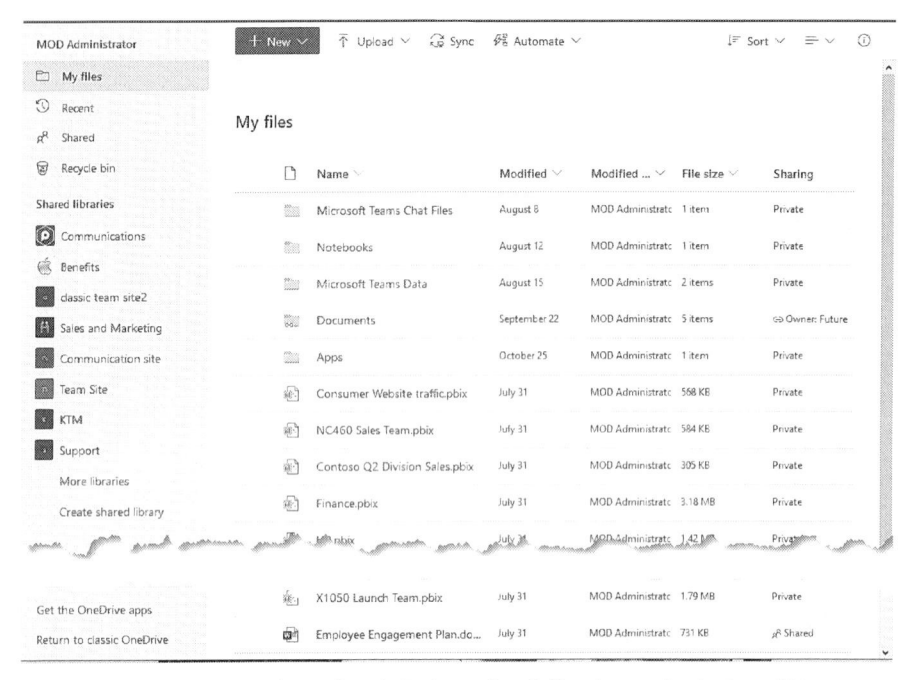

The left menu cannot be edited. It has the following tabs below "My files":

- Recently used files
- Shared files
- Recycle bin for OneDrive, where deleted content can be restored or permanently deleted
- Shared libraries: SharePoint document libraries that you have access to. Libraries that you have added a shortcut to are prominent here.
- More libraries: libraries you have access too, grouped by Frequent and Followed in the main area
- Create shared library: create a modern Group Team site, for collaboration or for your own use, *see* Create a Site below
- Get the OneDrive apps: get a download link to the Android or iOS OneDrive for Business mobile app
- Return to classic OneDrive: to show the library in the classic interface

7.2　User Settings

You can reach your personal OneDrive settings from the 365 Settings icon in the "My files" library.

Settings   ×

OneDrive

OneDrive settings

Restore your OneDrive

Here, you can turn off notifications and make some other settings that are available under the Site settings in standard SharePoint sites.

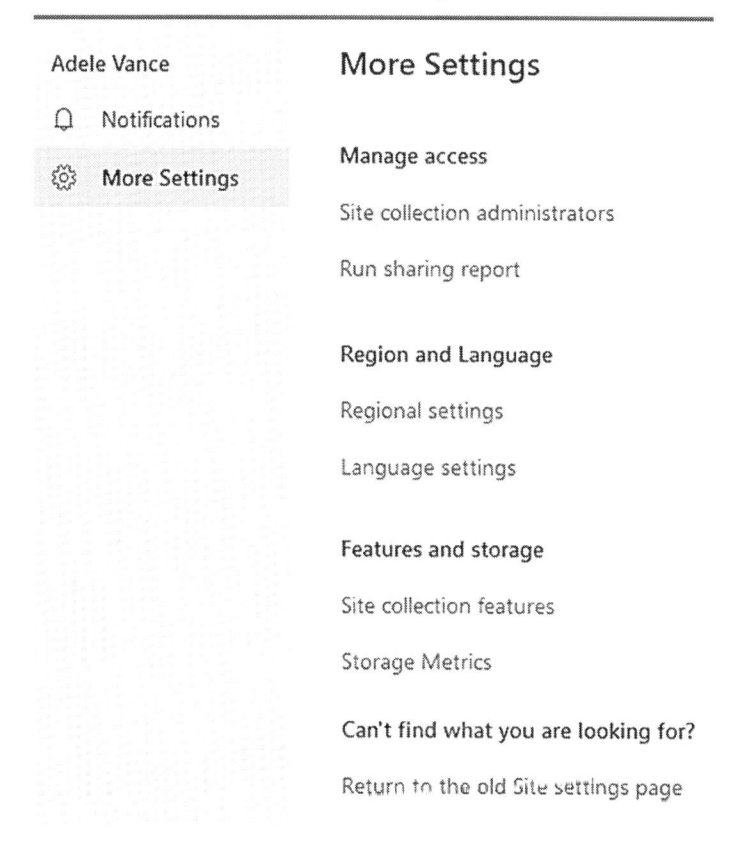

Adele Vance	**More Settings**
◯ Notifications	
⚙ **More Settings**	**Manage access**
	Site collection administrators
	Run sharing report
	Region and Language
	Regional settings
	Language settings
	Features and storage
	Site collection features
	Storage Metrics
	Can't find what you are looking for?
	Return to the old Site settings page

7.2.1 Restore OneDrive

You can restore your OneDrive to an earlier time, to undo unwanted changes:

1. In the OneDrive "My files" library, open the 365 Settings icon and select 'Restore your OneDrive'.

105

2. Select a date. (The date can be changed later, but you must select something to be able to go forward.)
3. Study the changes and move the slider to other days if necessary. The activity chart shows the volume of activities each day for the last 30 days, so that you easier can see when an unusual activity, like when your OneDrive was infected by malware, has happened.
4. Select an activity. All activities that occurred after that will be selected automatically.
5. Click on the Restore button, and your OneDrive will be restored to the selected activity. All activities after that will be undone.

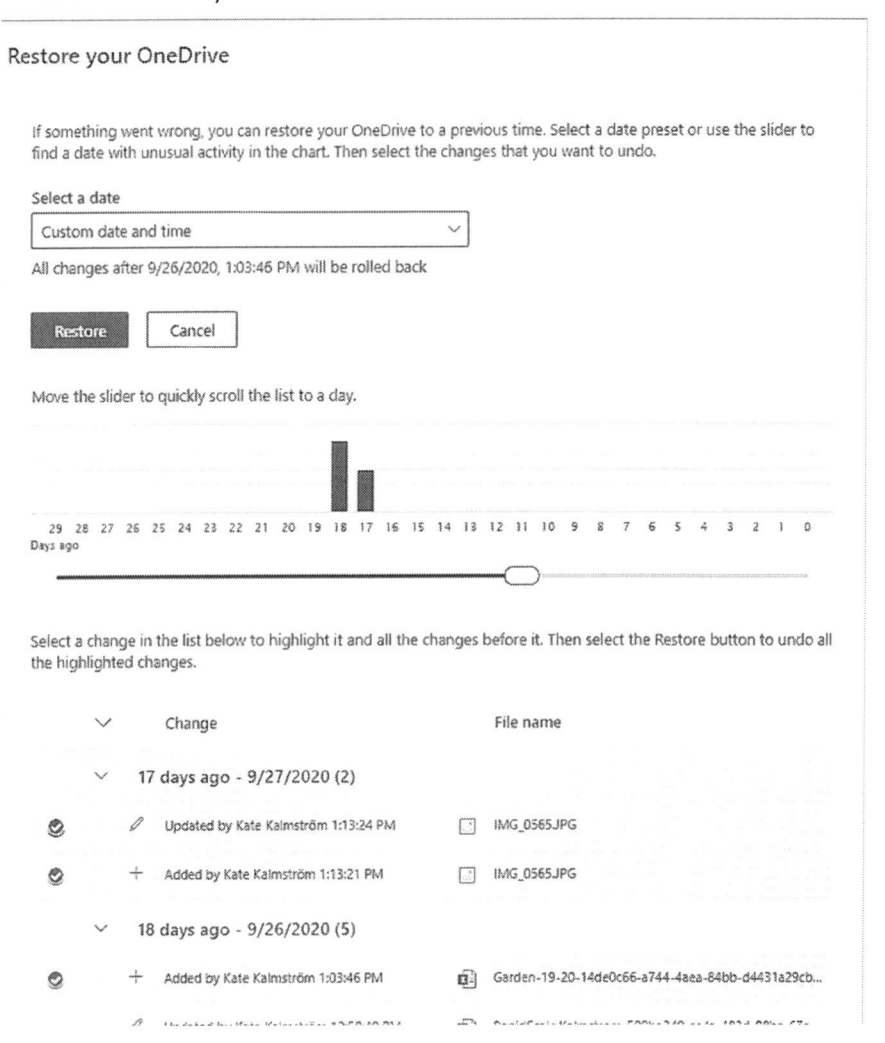

Restore your OneDrive

If something went wrong, you can restore your OneDrive to a previous time. Select a date preset or use the slider to find a date with unusual activity in the chart. Then select the changes that you want to undo.

Select a date

Custom date and time	∨

All changes after 9/26/2020, 1:03:46 PM will be rolled back

Restore   Cancel

Move the slider to quickly scroll the list to a day.

29 28 27 26 25 24 23 22 21 20 19 18 17 16 15 14 13 12 11 10 9 8 7 6 5 4 3 2 1 0
Days ago

Select a change in the list below to highlight it and all the changes before it. Then select the Restore button to undo all the highlighted changes.

	Change		File name
∨	17 days ago - 9/27/2020 (2)		
⊘	✎ Updated by Kate Kalmström 1:13:24 PM		IMG_0565.JPG
⊘	+ Added by Kate Kalmström 1:13:21 PM		IMG_0565.JPG
∨	18 days ago - 9/26/2020 (5)		
⊘	+ Added by Kate Kalmström 1:03:46 PM		Garden-19-20-14de0c66-a744-4aea-84bb-d4431a29cb...

7.3 Sharing from OneDrive

All files and folders that you store in OneDrive for Business are private until you decide to share them. To easily share files with different groups of people in your organization, you can place files that should be shared with the same people in folders and then share each folder.

The sharing is done with the 'Share' button or by sending a link, and it works in the same way as sharing a file from a SharePoint document library, *refer to* 9.4, Share a File.

You can manage the access in the same way as in a SharePoint document library too, but the "My files" library also has a "Sharing" column in the library interface. It has the value options 'Private' and 'Shared', and when you click on a 'Shared' value you can see and change access to the file.

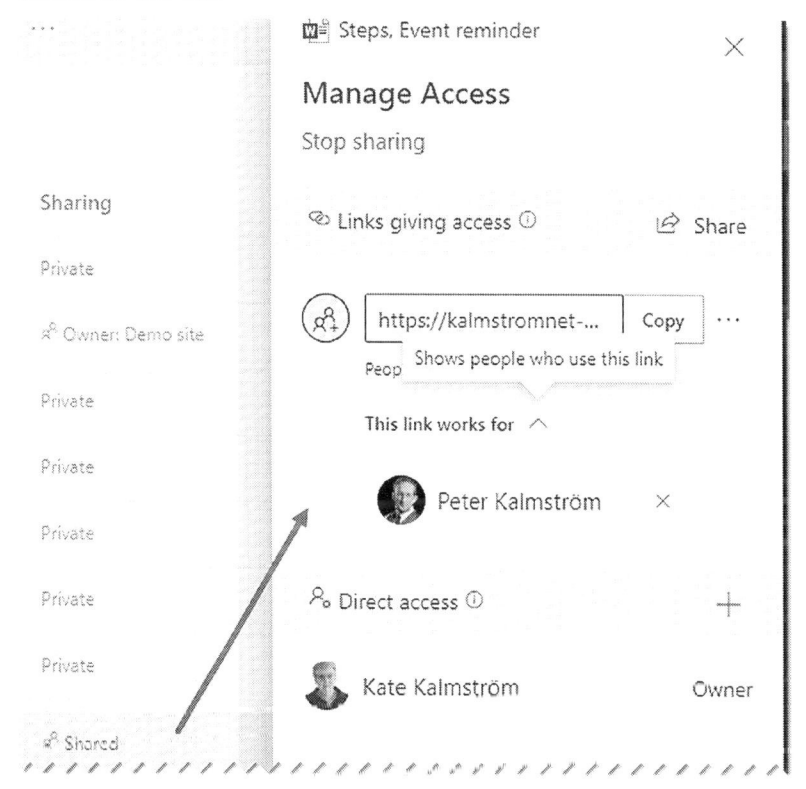

If you hover over the file name, you will see a card that shows information about the file and who has viewed it.

DetailedDescriptionShareTask.do...

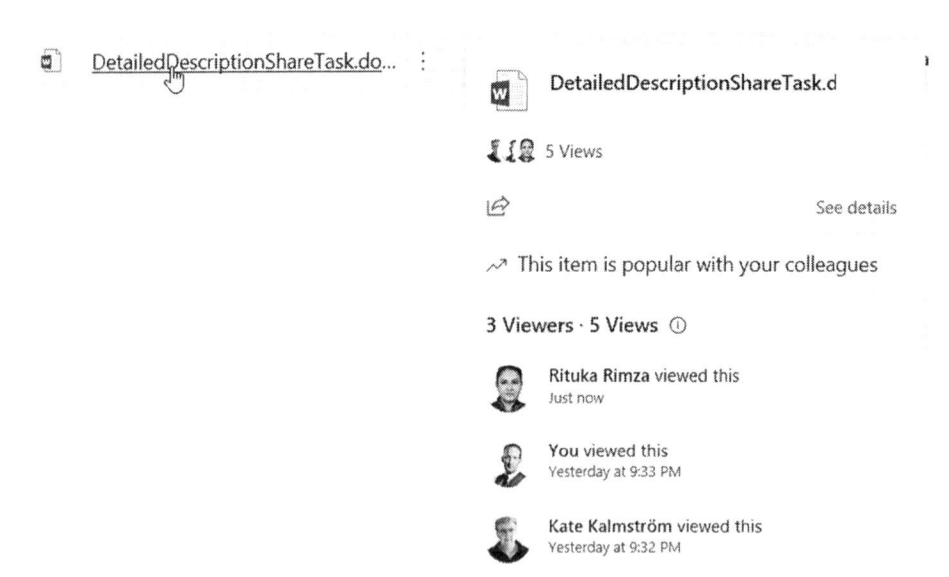

DetailedDescriptionShareTask.d

5 Views

See details

↗ This item is popular with your colleagues

3 Viewers · 5 Views

Rituka Rimza viewed this
Just now

You viewed this
Yesterday at 9:33 PM

Kate Kalmström viewed this
Yesterday at 9:32 PM

In your OneDrive settings, you can download a CSV file with sharing data. You can open this file in Excel.

7.4 SYNCHRONIZE WITH A LOCAL FOLDER

OneDrive for Business manages synchronization between files in SharePoint and a local File Explorer, so that you can add SharePoint and OneDrive document libraries (or library folders) as folders in your personal computer or smart device and edit them there.

You can also add new files to these synchronized library folders, and they will be uploaded to the library when you are signed in to SharePoint.

You can access the files even if you are offline, and they are synchronized automatically when you sign in to SharePoint again.

There is also a manual synchronization via the Sync button in the library command bar.

↻ Sync

In this section, I will describe how the synchronization between libraries and the File Explorer folders should be set up.

7.4.1 First Sync between a SharePoint Library and a Folder

Once you have set up the synchronization between a library and your device, OneDrive for Business will keep track of changes and synchronize this library and folder automatically.

However, the first time you must do it manually. You can also perform the steps below anytime, if you need to make a manual sync.

1. Open any SharePoint document library.
2. Click on the 'Sync' button in the command bar.
3. A 'Getting ready to sync' dialog will open. It has a link to download OneDrive for Business, but as it is included in the Office 365 subscription, you should not have to use that link.
4. You might be asked to open OneDrive for Business and/or to log in with your Office 365 account. Then you will see the location and name of your library folder that will be created on your computer. You now have a possibility to change the location.

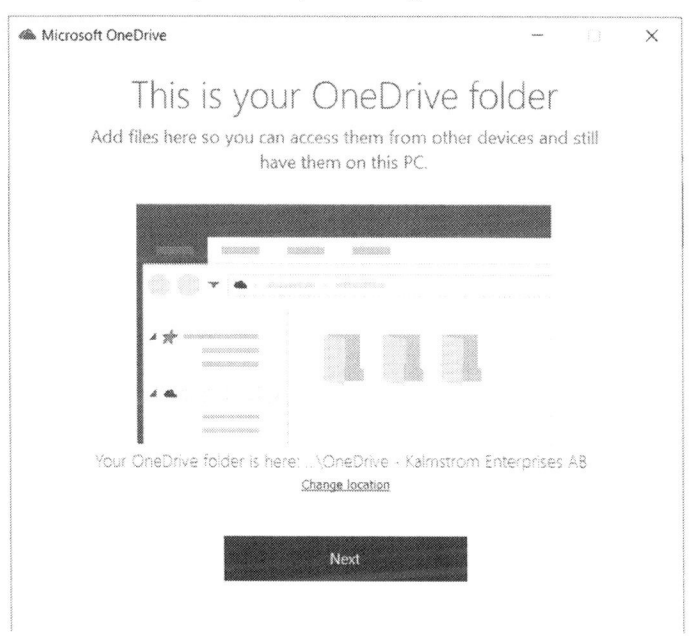

5. When you click on 'Next', you will get a presentation of OneDrive for Business in 6 screens. You will also have a possibility to download the OneDrive for Business mobile app.

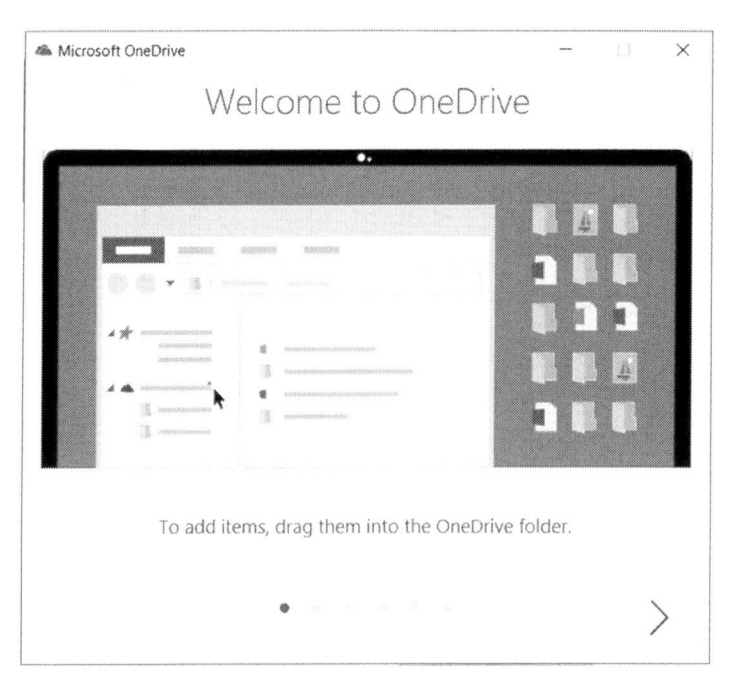

6. Then you are finished.

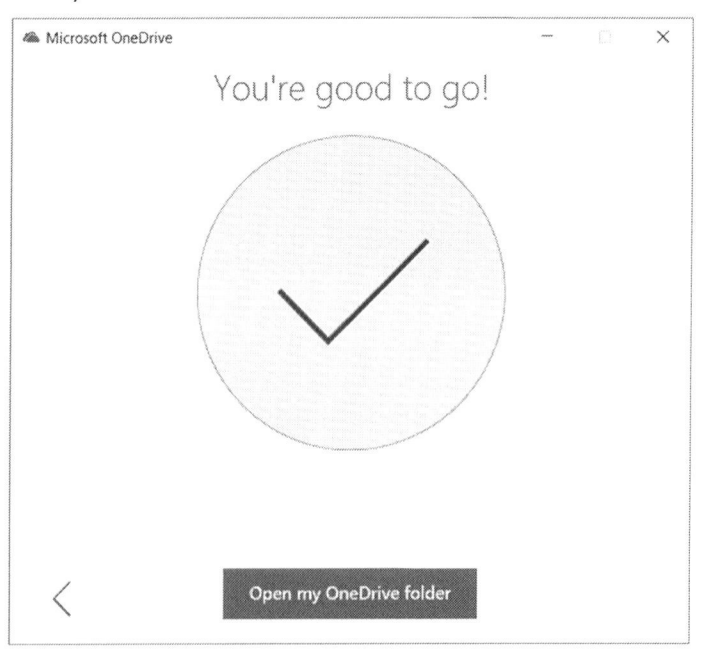

Now you have a new folder in your File Explorer. From now on, OneDrive for Business will keep track of changes and synchronize the library and folder automatically.

If you add the new library folder to your Favorites/Quick access, it will be smooth to move files between that folder and your other folders. When you drag or copy/cut and paste items to the synchronized library folder, they will be automatically uploaded to the library when you are online and logged in to Microsoft 365.

When you synchronize the OneDrive for Business "My files" library, the folder name will be OneDrive - COMPANY.

📁 OneDrive - Kalmstrom Enterprises AB

When you synchronize other SharePoint document libraries, they will be gathered as subfolders under a COMPANY folder. The subfolders have the names SITE - LIBRARY

📁 Kalmstrom Enterprises AB   📁 Sales - Sales Documents

7.4.2 Sync Issues

If the synchronization does not work, you can consider if one of these points can be the problem.

- The file is open.
- The file or folder name has a character that is not supported: \, /, :, *, ?, ", <, >, | , # , %,~.

7.4.3 Sync Settings

Click on the OneDrive icon in the task bar on your computer to reach the synchronization settings. (You might need to click on the 'Show hidden icons' arrow to see the OneDrive icon.)

7.4.3.1 Files On-Demand

OneDrive Files On-Demand is a feature that saves storage space on the computer, as it helps you access synchronized files without downloading all of them. The Files On-Demand setting is found under the Settings tab in the synchronization settings.

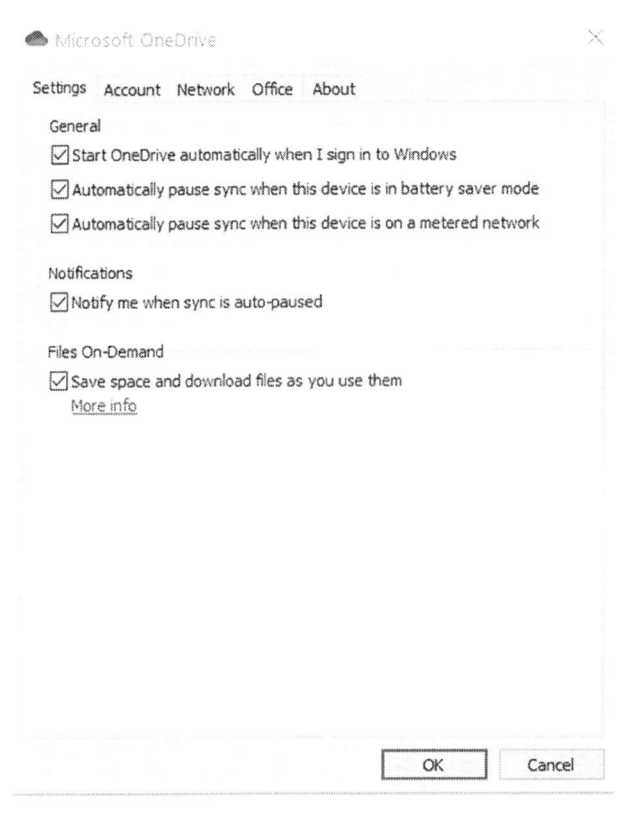

When the Settings box for 'Save space and download files as you use them' is checked, you can access your files without having to download them and take up storage space on your device:

Right-click on folders or files on your device and select either 'Always keep on this device' or 'Free up space'.

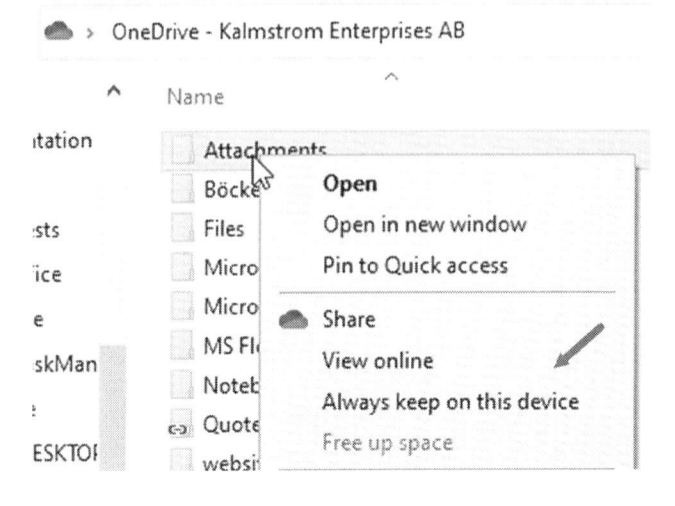

New files created online or on another device appear as online-only files, so they don't take up space on your device. When you are connected to the internet, you can use the online files like every other file on your device.

In your File Explorer, each synchronized file has a status icon that shows how the file is available. These are the icons, from top to bottom in the image to the right:

- Online-only: These files don't download to your device until you open them. You can only open these files when the device is connected to the internet.

- Locally available: When you open an online-only file, it downloads to your device and becomes a locally available file. Now you can open it anytime, even if you don't have internet access.

  These local files are cached, and if the drive gets low on space, some of the oldest files that have not been accessed in a while may be moved back to a cloud state to free up space. You can set this in Windows 10 under Storage >Change how we free up space automatically.

- Always keep: Files marked "Always Keep On Device" will always stay on the device and will not be moved back to cloud state automatically, even if drive space is low.

- Sync: synchronization is pending for the file.

7.5 CREATE A SITE

You cannot create new apps, pages or subsites from the "My files" library, but you can still get much better SharePoint functionality from OneDrive than what you have in the default library. Here, I will describe how you can create a Group Team site from OneDrive and either use it for yourself or invite other people to it.

When you click on "Create shared library" in the OneDrive left menu, you will get a simplified experience for creating a Group Team site.

In the image below, I have invited a few people and opened the advanced settings. If you want to use the site for yourself, you only need to enter a name and then click on 'Create'.

Create a shared library

A shared library lets your group store and access files from anywhere on any device. The group automatically gets access to the files that members put in the shared library.

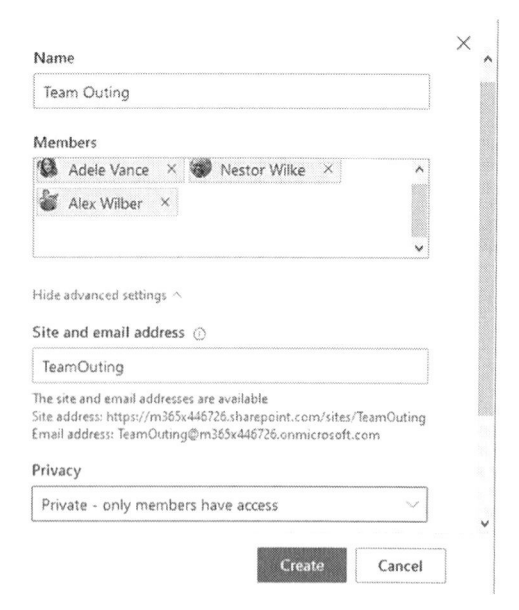

Name

Team Outing

Members

Adele Vance ×   Nestor Wilke ×
Alex Wilber ×

Hide advanced settings ∧

Site and email address ⓘ

TeamOuting

The site and email addresses are available
Site address: https://m365x446726.sharepoint.com/sites/TeamOuting
Email address: TeamOuting@m365x446726.onmicrosoft.com

Privacy

Private - only members have access

[Create] [Cancel]

When the site has been created, the new document library will be displayed as a folder in the OneDrive for Business main area. Click on the folder to open the document library. This library is also limited compared to SharePoint document libraries, even if it has some more features than the "My files" library.

The important thing here is the link to the SharePoint site in the top right corner of the page. Except for the limited "Documents" library, what you have created is a full Group Team site.

If you create a new document library from the site's homepage, it will have all the features of other SharePoint document libraries. You can of course also create other apps and pages.

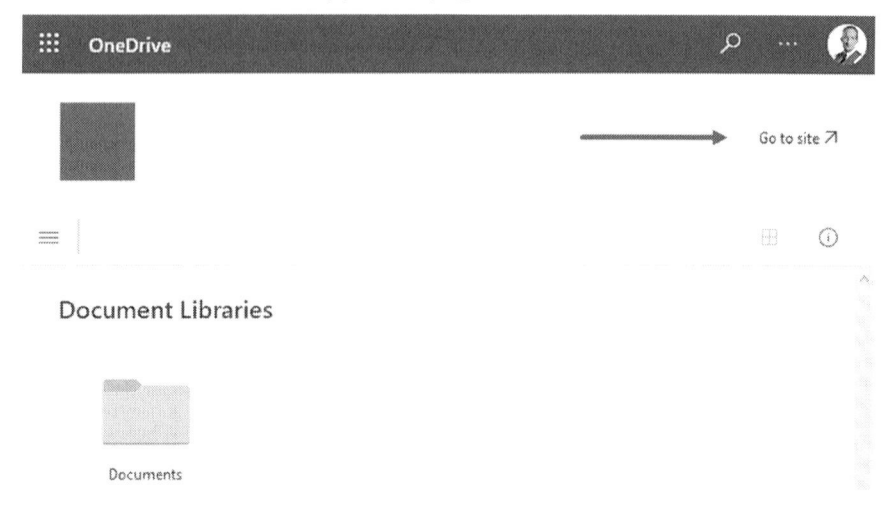

::: OneDrive

⟶ Go to site ↗

Document Libraries

Documents

When you have clicked on 'Go to site' and the site opens, be sure to click on 'Not following' to follow the new site. Now, the site will show up on your SharePoint start page, and the document library can be found under 'Shared libraries' in the OneDrive for Business left menu.

7.6 Multiple Libraries Benefits

One way of taking advantage of your Group Team site, is to create multiple libraries. This gives important advantages and lets you share and synchronize in a more controlled way than if you use only the default OneDrive for Business library:

- SharePoint does not work well when you have more than 5000 files in a library. If you create more libraries in your site, you will overcome that problem.
- You can share different libraries with different groups of people.
- You can sync different libraries with different devices.
- When you create several libraries, you can choose to not synchronize all of them to your device. The libraries you don't synchronize, can be used for storage of files that you don't need to access very often.

7.7 Summary

As you already know, SharePoint is primarily a platform for sharing, but included in you SharePoint Online account is also OneDrive for Business, which gives you a personal space in the cloud.

In this chapter, I have introduced the default OneDrive for Business document library, and I have also explained how you can use OneDrive to create more apps, pages and sites.

OneDrive for Business also manages the synchronization of library items between your computer and SharePoint or OneDrive. In this chapter, you have learned how this synchronization works and how to set it up.

Finally, I have explained how to restore OneDrive and how the default OneDrive library is adapted to sharing. We will come back to the sharing in chapter 9, but before that we will take a look at the SharePoint site pages.

8 SITE PAGES

As we have seen earlier, SharePoint sites can store a lot of various content, and all content that should be visible to users is displayed on pages inside a site.

Each page is an ASPX file, which you can see on the URL. We have already talked about the homepage of a site. Its URL ends with Home.aspx, and each page that you create yourself ends with the page name + .aspx.

Some SharePoint pages are created automatically, for example settings pages and app pages. These pages cannot be customized at all in SharePoint Online. (You can customize an app, but not the page it is contained in.)

Homepages are also created automatically, but they can – and should – be customized. Pages that can be customized are called site pages.

Site pages can contain many kinds of content. In this chapter, I will describe how you can create site pages and add content to them.

By default, all users except visitors can create and customize the pages described in this chapter This possibility can be disabled for all sites in the SharePoint Admin center, and each site owner can also deactivate the possibility to create pages for one site. This is done under Site settings >Manage site features >Site pages.

The most common reason for creating a new page is probably that you need to have an additional space for some specific content. Instead of adding the content to an existing page, it is often better to create a new page for it. If you give a good name to the page, the content will be easier to find than if you add it to a page that already has other content.

In some cases, it might be better to create a page than to create a document. Pages are easier to read than documents, and pages load quicker and can contain videos.

In this chapter, you will learn how to:

- Open a page in edit mode.
- Add and edit pages and web parts.
- Save and publish page modifications.

We will however start with an introduction to the library where the pages are stored.

8.1 THE "SITE PAGES" LIBRARY

SharePoint pages are files, and site pages are stored in the site's "Site Pages" library. You can reach this library from the Site contents, and often also via a 'Pages' link in the Site navigation.

The "Site Pages" library is created automatically when you create a new site. Generally, it works in the same way as a document library, but there are no buttons for upload or download.

Site owners can add extra columns to the "Site Pages" library, to categorize the pages with metadata, and they can make columns mandatory to fill out. If a mandatory property is missing at publishing, the page author will have a message about it, and the page cannot be published until the mandatory property has been filled out.

The page properties can be managed in the "Site Pages" library in the same way as file properties in a document library. The properties can also be seen and edited directly on the page, via the 'Page details' button in the command bar.

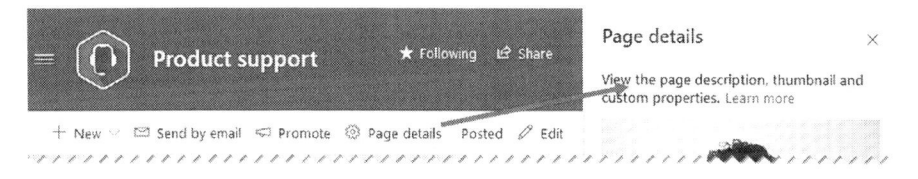

8.1.1 Check Out

Conflicting situations, where several people edit the same page, cannot occur in modern pages, because they are checked out automatically when someone opens the page in edit mode.

Users who start editing a modern page, can see if someone else is already editing the same page, who that person is and how to contact him/her.

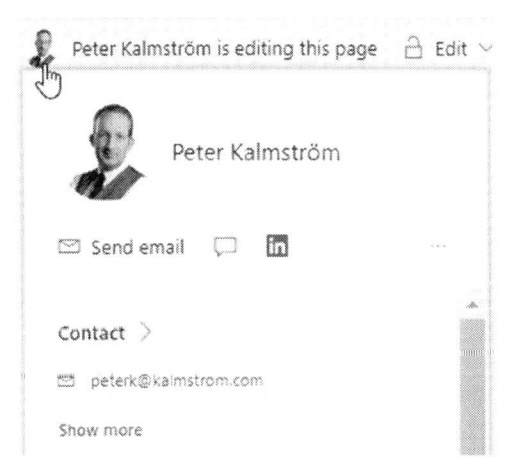

The page cannot be edited, but the site owner can discard the other person's changes.

In the "Site Pages" library, an icon shows that the page is checked out, just like in document libraries.

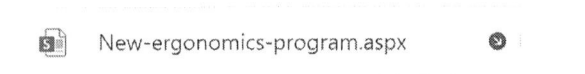

New-ergonomics-program.aspx

8.1.2 Version History

Just as document libraries, the "Site Pages" library has version history enabled by default. It gives a possibility to restore earlier page versions and works just as described in section 3.10.

There is also a link to the page's Version history in the 'Page details' pane.

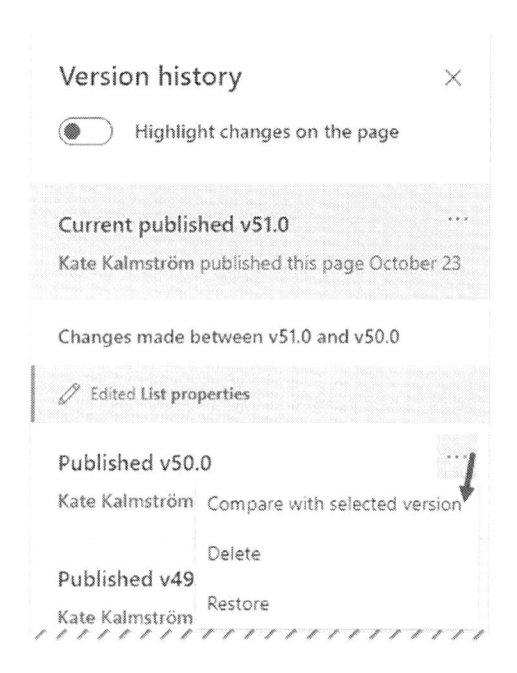

Version history

Highlight changes on the page

Current published v51.0
Kate Kalmström published this page October 23

Changes made between v51.0 and v50.0

Edited **List properties**

Published v50.0
Kate Kalmström   Compare with selected version
                 Delete
Published v49
                 Restore
Kate Kalmström

8.1.3 Scheduled Page Publishing

The command bar in the "Site Pages" library has a 'Scheduling' button. It opens a right pane where you can enable scheduling for the site.

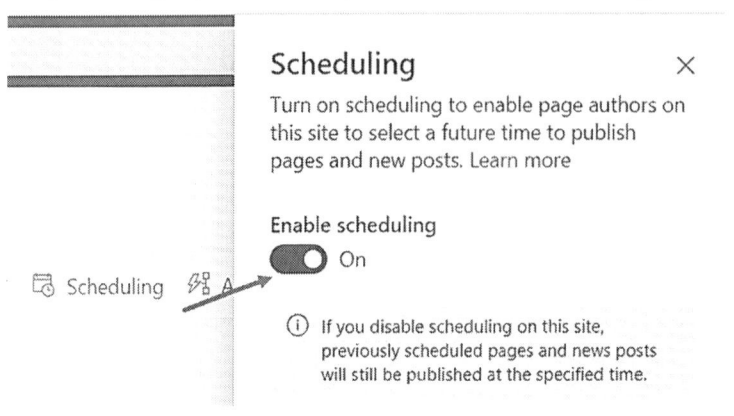

Scheduling

Scheduling

Turn on scheduling to enable page authors on this site to select a future time to publish pages and new posts. Learn more

Enable scheduling
On

ⓘ If you disable scheduling on this site, previously scheduled pages and news posts will still be published at the specified time.

118

When scheduling has been enabled in the "Site Pages" library, page creators can schedule the publishing of new or modified pages, if needed. This is done in the page's "Page details" pane.

With the page in edit mode, open the page details and set the Scheduling toggle to On. Now you can select a date and a time for the publishing.

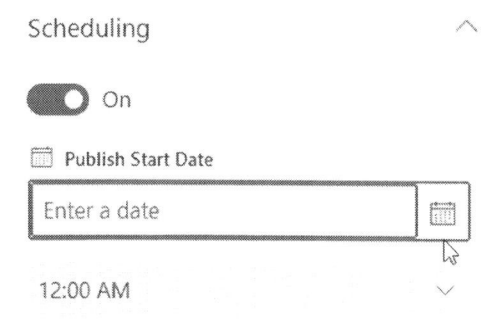

Scheduling

On

Publish Start Date

Enter a date

12:00 AM

8.1.4 Copy a Page

In the "Site Pages" library, you can use the 'Copy to' command that I earlier described for libraries to copy a page with all its content and layout.

The page will be copied to the same "Site Pages" library, so that you can use the page as a template for another page in the site.

1. Select the page file you want to copy.
2. Click on 'Copy to' in the command bar or under the item ellipsis.
3. Click on 'Copy here' in the right pane (it is not possible to change the destination location).

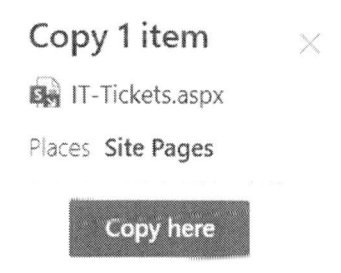

Copy 1 item

IT-Tickets.aspx

Places **Site Pages**

Copy here

4. The page will be copied and named with the suffix "1" after the original page name.
5. Select the new page, click on the ellipsis and rename the page.

8.1.5 Set a Page as Homepage

From the "Site Pages" library, you can easily replace a site's homepage with another page from the same site.

1. Select the page you want to set as the site's homepage.
2. Click on the ellipsis in the command bar or at the page file. S
3. Click on 'Make homepage'.

8.2 CREATE A PAGE

Site pages can be created from the "Site Pages" library.

When you click on '+ New' in a Team site, you can create several types of site pages. Select 'Site Page' to create the modern page I describe in this chapter.

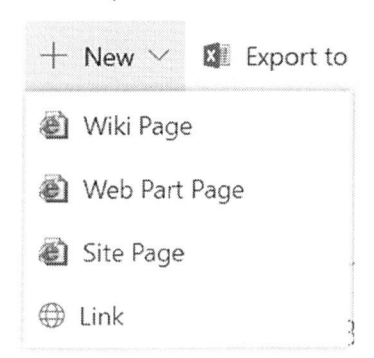

Communication sites only give the 'Site Page' and 'Link' options. (The 'Link' option adds a link to the "Site Pages" library, in the same way as in document libraries.)

You can also create modern site pages outside the "Site Pages" library:

- Click on the 365 Settings icon and select 'Add a page'.

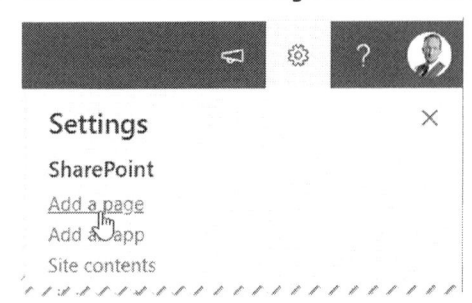

- In a modern homepage or in the modern 'Site contents' interface, click on '+ New' and select 'Page'.

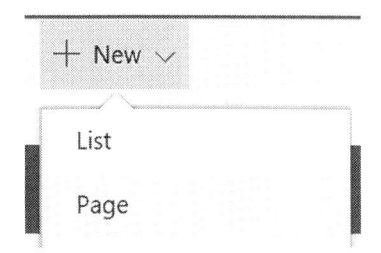

- In an existing modern page, click on '+ New' and select 'Page' or 'Copy of this page'.

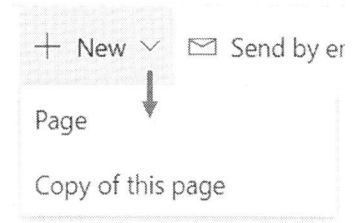

Modern pages are customized with web parts that cannot be used in other types of pages. These web parts can be combined on the page to make it interesting and useful.

Microsoft is planning to implement a tour the first time a user creates a new page or news post, to show how to pick a template, add and edit sections and web parts, title the page, and choose a title image. Maybe it is already implemented when you read this!

8.2.1 Page Templates

When you have begun creating a modern page in one of the ways described above, a right pane will open where you will have a choice of templates. Select the template you want to use and click on 'Create page'.

By default, a blank page is pre-selected, but site owners can make another template pre-selected via the ellipsis on the template card.

From the template card ellipsis, you can also open the template, and custom templates can be edited or deleted from the site.

The custom templates are only displayed on the site where the page was saved as a template, and they can only be used there.

The Built-in templates are displayed in all sites. They cannot be edited or removed, so the ellipsis dropdown only shows the option 'Set default selection'.

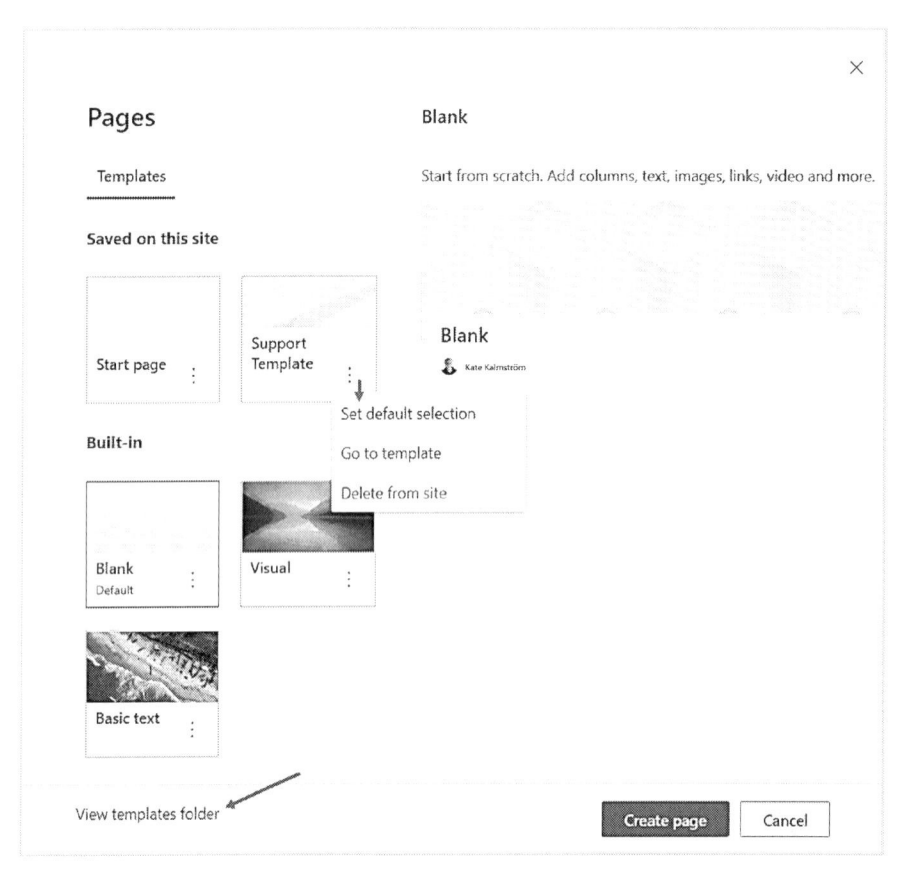

When you have selected your template, the new page will open in edit mode.

8.2.1.1 Save a Page as a Template

When you have created a page, you can let other people who have access to the site use your page as a template.

When you do that, the template will show up among the other templates when users create new modern pages.

To save a page as a temple, click on the 'Promote' button in the command bar when the page is in view mode and select the template option.

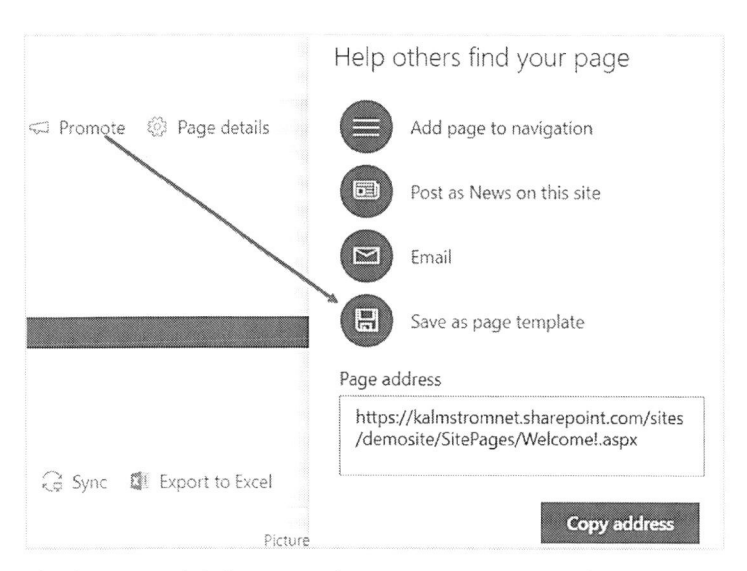

The 'Promote' right pane also opens automatically when you publish a page.

8.2.2 Edit Mode

To open an existing modern page in edit mode, click on the Edit button to the right in the command bar.

When the page is open in edit mode, there will instead be a 'Publish' button to the right in the command bar. Use it to publish your modifications, so that other users can see them.

After the first publication, the button text is 'Republish' when you edit the page again.

The page in edit mode has a title area on top, a canvas for the web parts below the title area and panes for web part editing that open to the right.

When you are working with the page, the command bar has an option to undo or redo recent modifications.

When the page has been published before, you can also select to discard all changes and go back to the earlier version of the page.

123

Use the 'Save as draft' button to see how the page looks for users or to continue working with the page on another occasion.

8.2.3 Title Area

Change the text at 'Name your page' in the title area of the new page. That text will be used to give the page a name.

You can rename the page later, but the original name will be kept in the page URL. Therefore, you should think twice before you give the page a name, so that you don't need to change it!

No styles can be applied in the title area, but there are some limited customization options. The toolbar with these options appears when you hover over the top left corner of the title area. Here, you can change the background image and reset the default image.

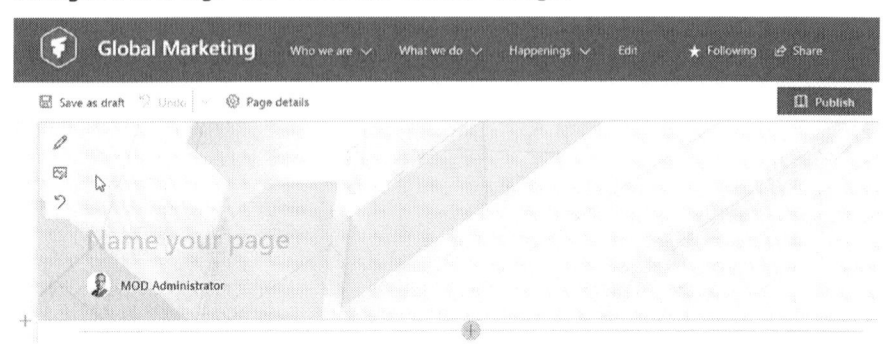

When you click on the edit icon in the title area toolbar, a right pane will open. Here, you can make some modifications to the area.

Select the 'Plain' option if you don't want to use a background image at all.

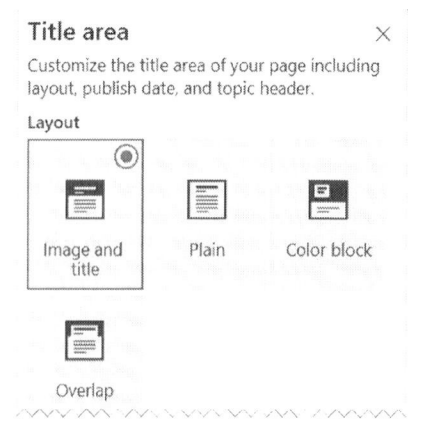

8.2.4 Comments

By default, the modern page has a Comments section at the bottom. It can be removed with the toggle to the right of the text 'Comments' when the page is in edit mode.

When a modern page is made into a homepage, the comments section will be disabled automatically on that page.

8.2.5 Sections

To organize the content on a modern page, you should use the sections feature to compose a nice-looking page.

To show the layout options, click on the plus sign to the left under the title area or under an existing section. The One column section is default.

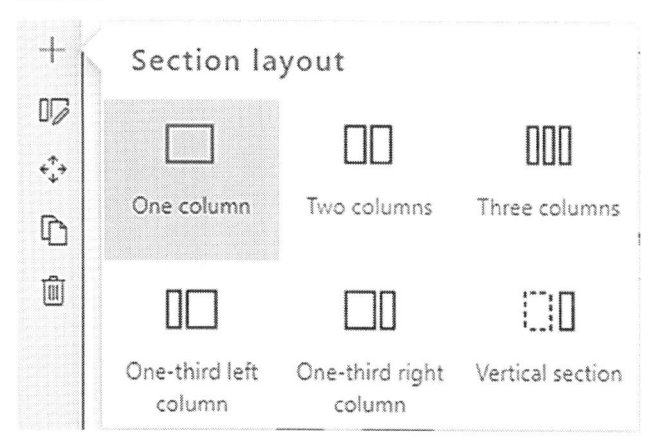

A section can have one, two or three columns. Each column can hold one or multiple web parts.

With the option 'Vertical section', you can add a new column to the right that will run along all the other sections.

The image above comes from a Group Team site. Communication sites have an additional option: a full-width column, where the layout expands to the full width of the page.

A page often has several sections, and each section can have its own color and layout. Just click on the left plus sign again to add a new section.

SharePoint automatically adds a text web part to each column when you add a new section, but if no text is entered, this text web part will not be visible on the published page.

8.2.6   Edit Sections and Web Parts

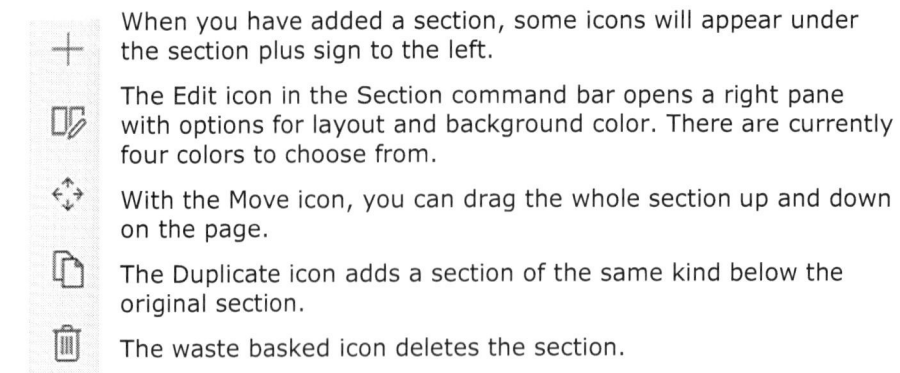

When you have added a section, some icons will appear under the section plus sign to the left.

The Edit icon in the Section command bar opens a right pane with options for layout and background color. There are currently four colors to choose from.

With the Move icon, you can drag the whole section up and down on the page.

The Duplicate icon adds a section of the same kind below the original section.

The waste basked icon deletes the section.

When you add web parts to the section columns, the same kind of icons will appear to the left of the web part when you select it. Here, the commands apply to the web part and not to the section. The content in the right Edit pane is different for each web part.

8.2.7   Add Web Parts

The modern site page gives a choice of dedicated web parts that can be added to the page. Some web parts allow extensive customization, but many of them only have a few options.

When you have added a section to the page, it is time to start adding web parts to the section. Click on the plus sign in the middle of a column to show the web part selection.

Start typing in the Search box to easily find the web part you are looking for.

You can also search for web parts by category, and there is a toggle to switch between grid view and a list view with web part descriptions. Your most frequently used web parts will be shown on top.

Add the web part you prefer to the page by clicking on its icon.

Search				
		Filter by Category ∨		

Frequently used

Text	Image	File viewer	Link	Embed

Text and formatting

Text	Button	Call to action	Link	Spacer

—	⊕			

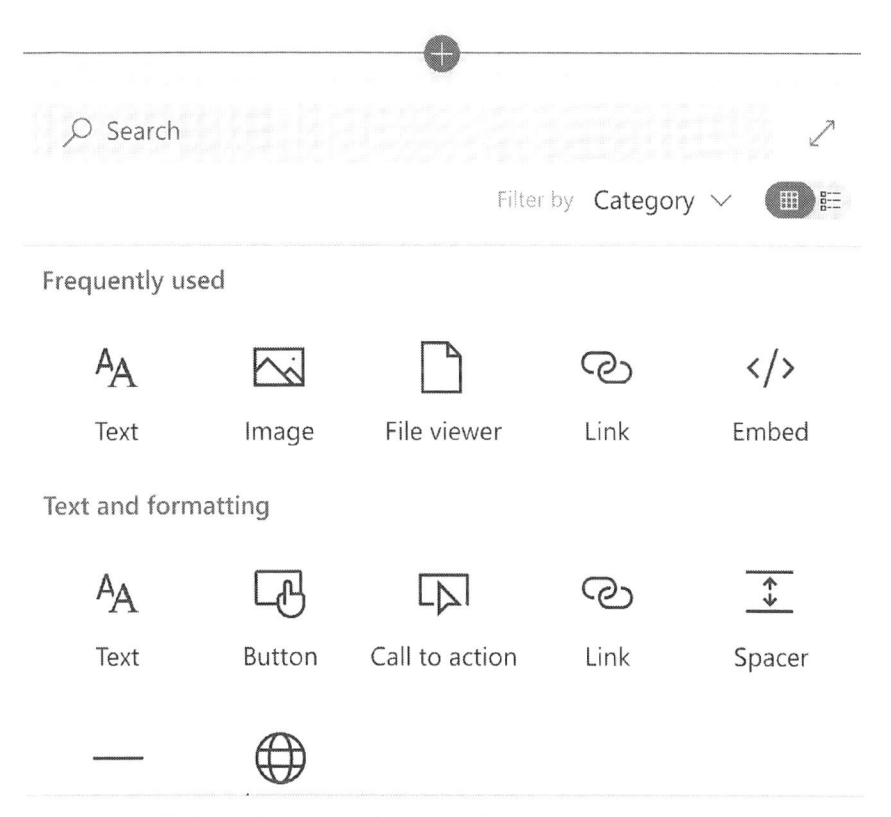

When you click on the expand icon in the top right corner of the small web part selector, you will see a larger view of the web parts.

When you have added and edited the web part, you can add more web parts in the same section or add a new section to add more web parts below or above the first section.

You can also anytime add new sections and web parts between existing sections and web parts.

8.2.8   Add Content to Web Parts

Most web parts are empty until you fill them with a specified kind of content. This content is linked to the web part, not added directly on the page. All content is governed by permissions, so users will only see what they have access to.

When you upload content from your computer to a web part, everyone who has access to the page will also get access to the content from your computer.

Uploaded content will be added to a "SitePages" folder in the site's "Site Assets" library. Each page will have its own folder inside the "SitePages" folder.

Most often, your changes to the web part will be saved automatically, but if you see an 'Apply' button at the bottom of the right Edit pane you should click on it!

In many web parts, the content is added in one these ways:

- The web part opens with a field where the content, for example text or a link, can be added directly into the web part.
- The web part and the right Edit pane opens at the same time.
- When you have clicked on the web part to add it to the page, a wide, right pane for location selection opens. Here you can find a menu to the left and content options to the right.

  - Recent
  - Stock images
  - Web search
  - OneDrive
  - Site
  - Upload
  - From a link

  The left location menu is the same in most web parts. Select a link in the left hand menu and then select the content you want to add from the main area to the right (except for the Upload option, which opens your File Explorer).

- The web part opens on the page, and you can add content by clicking on a button in the web part. When you do that, either the location selection pane or the right Edit pane opens, so that you can make your choices.

You can also always select the web part to display the left command bar, *see* above in 8.2.6, Edit Sections and Web Parts. Click on the pen icon to edit the web part or replace the content.

8.2.8.1 Add Image or File

When you want to add just one image to a page, you should use the Image web part, and for just one file you should use the File Viewer web part.

When you use these web parts, you don't have to add the web part to the page first. You can just drag the image or file to the canvas area when the page is in edit mode.

Drop the file when you see a line on the page. Now the Image or File viewer web part will be added automatically, filled with the image or file that you dragged to the page.

8.2.9   Web Part Examples

When this is written, Microsoft supplies 46 web parts to use with modern pages, and new web parts are published continuously. In addition to that, each tenant can have third party apps that have been added to the organization's App Catalog and are available for the whole tenant.

Most web parts have names that tell what they can display, and they are not difficult to figure out. Therefore, I will not go into each of them here but just give a few examples on how you can use modern web parts.

Should you need assistance, Microsoft has a good online guide where most modern web parts are described in detail:
https://support.office.com/en-us/article/Using-web-parts-on-SharePoint-Online-pages-336e8e92-3e2d-4298-ae01-d404bbe751e0

The web part setting options I describe in the sections below are set in the right pane that opens when you edit the web part.

8.2.9.1   365 Apps

Several 365 apps and services have their own modern web parts, where you can display content that has been created with the apps. Such web parts are Bing maps, Group calendar, Microsoft Forms, Microsoft Stream, Power BI and Yammer conversations and highlights.

8.2.9.2   Button and Call to action

The Button and Call to action web parts let you create a button that loads the content you specify with a link.

8.2.9.3   Divider

The Divider web part is simply a vertical line that divides web parts. Its color follows the theme of the site, but you can control the length and to some extent also the thickness.

8.2.9.4   Document Library and List

The Document library and List web parts show the library or list you select (only from within the site). These web parts don't have all the features that are present in the apps, but for many purposes the existing features are enough to work with the app.

When you have added the web part to the page, the names of the libraries or lists in the site will be loaded to the web part, so that you can select one of them to display.

In the Document library web part, all libraries in the site will show up for selection, not only document libraries. Therefore, you can add other kinds of libraries to this web part too, for example a Picture library, *refer to* 8.4, Add Images to Pages.

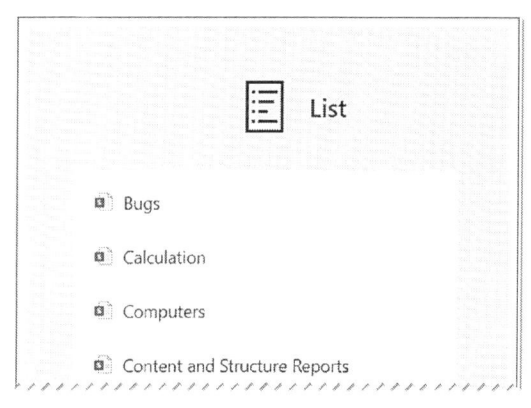

With list apps, it is the other way around. When this is written, you can only add custom list apps and lists built on the Announcements, Contacts and Issue tracking templates to the Lists web part.

When you add a Document library or List web part to a page, files and items can be opened directly from the page. You can also do much other work without leaving the page. You can for example switch view and open the grid, and when you select an item and click on the Information icon, the right pane will open in edit mode so that you can edit the metadata.

New items can be created, and in the library web part, files can be uploaded or downloaded.

8.2.9.5 Hero

The Hero web part is by default added to the homepage of a new Topic and Showcase Communication site, but you can add it to other modern pages too.

In the Hero web part, you can add up to five items in tiles or layers and use images and text to draw attention to each of them.

Videos can also be added, but they are not played on the page. Instead, users are taken to the video player or link source when they click on the video tile.

In the right Edit pane for the Hero web part, you can select several layout options.

When you have chosen layout, add the items by clicking on the 'Select link' buttons. Then you can edit each item with the icons you see when you hover over a tile.

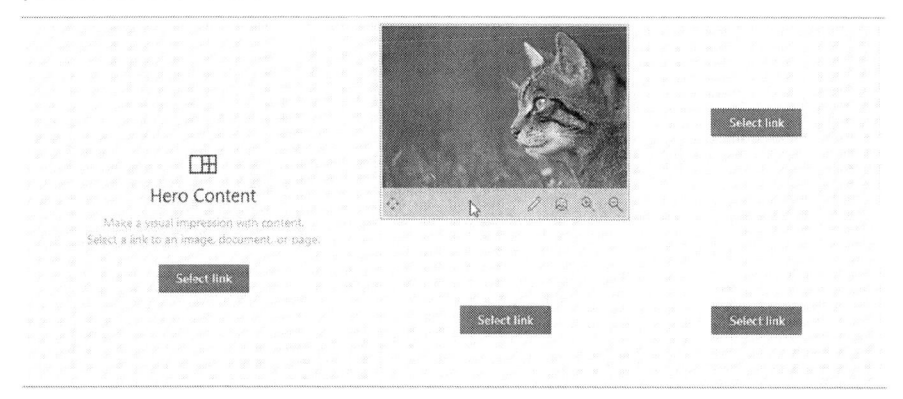

From left to right, the icons on the tiles let you:

- Open the right pane to edit the tile.
- Move the item. Select with the icon and then use Ctrl + left or right arrow to move.
- Set the focal point of the tile.
- Enlarge or decrease what is shown in the tile.

The right Edit pane for each item gives options for text and settings. It is also here you can change the item in the tile or layer.

8.2.9.6 Highlighted Content

The Highlighted content web part uses the search engine to get content. By default, it searches for and displays your most recently used content in the site, but you can customize what the web part should search for and display.

As the web part uses the search engine, all content will be security trimmed and users will only be shown content that they have access to.

The Highlighted content web part can also filter and sort the items, and you can select layout and decide how many items should be displayed.

With the Highlighted Content web part you are invited to specify source, content type and metadata, and the web part will show items according to that.

This means that you must in some way narrow the search to display exactly the content you want to show. You can, for example:

- keep the content you wish to display in a specific document library
- select to show a certain kind of content type, for example videos or documents
- give a specific keyword to each item you want to include

8.2.9.7 Spacer

The Spacer web part gives a horizontal space that divides sections or web parts. It is possible to change the size by dragging the bottom line up and down. You can also use the arrow keys.

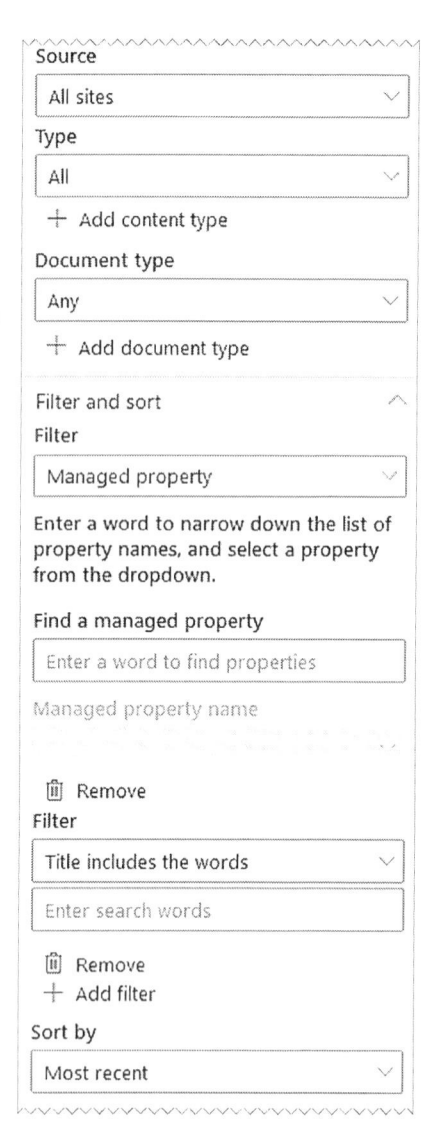

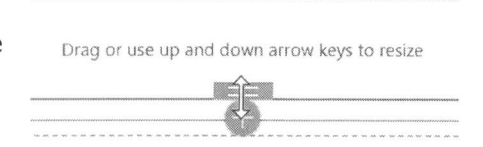

8.2.10   Page Details

When you click on the Page details button in the modern page command bar when the page is in Edit mode, you can add a description and a custom thumbnail for the page. These will be shown in the SharePoint search results and news.

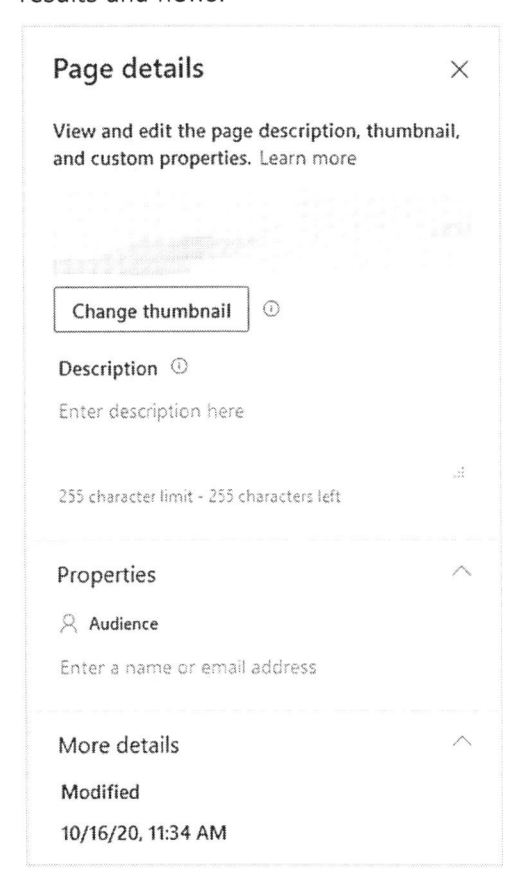

⚙ Page details

Page details   ✕

View and edit the page description, thumbnail, and custom properties. Learn more

[Change thumbnail] ⓘ

Description ⓘ

Enter description here

255 character limit - 255 characters left

Properties   ∧

👤 Audience

Enter a name or email address

More details   ∧

Modified

10/16/20, 11:34 AM

When the page has been published, the Page details pane shows the same information, but now you can also find a link to the Version history for the page, below the Modified information.

The Version history link opens another right pane, where you can compare versions and restore or delete earlier versions.

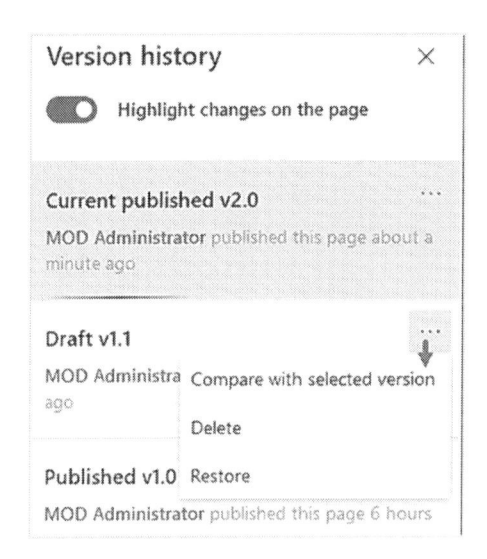

8.2.11 Promote a Page

The 'Promote' right pane, gives several options for sharing information about the page.

This pane opens when you publish a page and when you click on the 'Promote' button in the command bar.

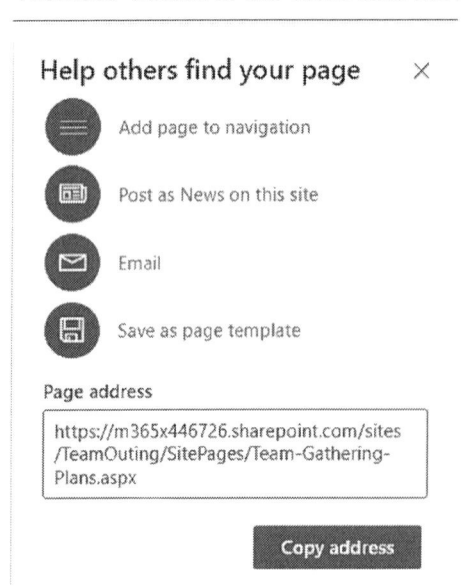

You can also promote the page via the e-mail button in the command bar.

Also *refer to* 9.5, Share a Page.

8.2.12 The News Web Part

When you add a News web part to a page, you only select the source(s) for the news and decide the layout. The actual content in the News web part comes when you and other users start creating news posts.

News posts can come from the site, from all sites in the hub or from one or more individual sites.

You can also choose the option 'Recommended for current user', which displays different posts for each user: from people the user works with, managers and connections and followed and frequently visited sites.

News Source

Select a news source

○ This site

◉ All sites in the hub

○ Select sites

○ Recommended for current user

You can select from multiple layouts for the News web part. The default layout depends on what kind of site the page is created in.

By default, the News web part shows the news posts in the order they are published, with the most recent on the prominent place, but you can reorder them by drag and drop under 'News Order' in the right Edit pane. The News web part also has many other settings in the right pane.

A News web part is added to the site's homepage when you create a Group Team site and a Topic Communication site.

8.2.12.1 Create a News Post

News posts are modern SharePoint pages. They are shown and can be managed in the "Site Pages" library, and they are created in the same way as other modern pages. The only difference is how you start creating them.

News posts can be created from the SharePoint Online start page.

A right pane will open, where you must select site where the news post should be posted. Then a blank modern page will open, and you can start creating the page with any web parts you wish to use.

When you are done with creating your new post, click on 'Post news' to the right in the command bar to publish it.

The news post will now be published to the site you selected and to other pages with a News web part that fetches news posts from that site.

News posts can also be created from the '+ New' button in modern homepages and from the 'Add' dropdown in a News web part.

In this case, you will have a possibility to select template before you start editing the page.

There is no site selection here. The post will be published to the News web part on the current site and to other pages with a News web part that fetches news posts from that site.

8.2.12.2 Create a News Link

As you see from the images above, it is possible to add a news post via a link to content inside or outside the tenant. The content you link to will be displayed as a news post.

In this case, you don't have to create a new page. All the editing is performed in a right pane, which also has a 'Post' button.

When you select 'News link' option from the '+ New' button in a modern homepage or from the 'Add' dropdown in a News web part, a right pane will open where you can paste the link.

When the link is added, a preview of the content is loaded, and a title and a description are suggested. You can of course change the preview image and edit the title and description before you post the news.

8.2.13 Spaces

Microsoft has very recently introduced a new kind of modern page called Space. It is so new that your tenant might not even have it if you read this book before mid-April 2021.

A space page is very graphic, with a possibility to add 2D and 3D web parts and to rotate the page 360°.

Creation of space pages is enabled by default, but it might be disabled for the tenant. Site owners can also disable Spaces under Site settings >Site Actions >Manage site features.

If allowed, you can create a space from the '+New' buttons in homepages and "Site Pages" libraries.

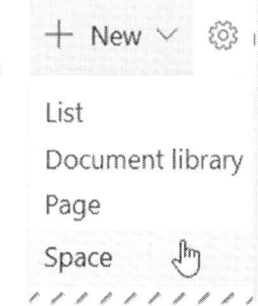

When you create a space, you can select a structure, a background image and ambient sound, and you can add an audio file with a recorded welcoming message.

The web parts are few, so far, and they remind of the other modern web parts – but when you add them to the page, you will see a difference.

You can add the web parts anywhere around the 360° area, and they are minimized until you click on one of them to bring it to the front – as I have done with a document in the image below.

When you understand how to create modern pages, the spaces are not difficult to figure out. Therefore, I will not go into space pages more deeply here.

8.3 Add Links to a Page

Links can be added to pages in many ways. Pages must always be in edit mode when links are added.

Modern pages have two web parts dedicated to links, Links and Quick Links. It is also possible to add links in some other web parts, like the Hero, Button, Call to action and Sites web parts, and to link text in the Text web part.

8.3.1 The Link Web Part

In the Link web part, you can paste any link directly into the web part. If available, a preview of the item will be displayed. You can only add one link to each Link web part.

8.3.2 The Quick Links Web Part

The Quick Links web part is more of a "pin" tool where you can add multiple links. Click on '+Add links' in the web part to add a link. You will have a choice of multiple places to get the link from.

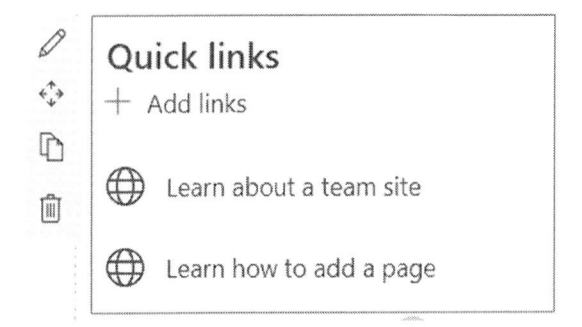

There are several layout options, but some of them are only for links from SharePoint. Select the web part and click on the Edit web part pen icon to select layout.

The image below shows a page where the Quick Links web part has been used with the Tile layout.

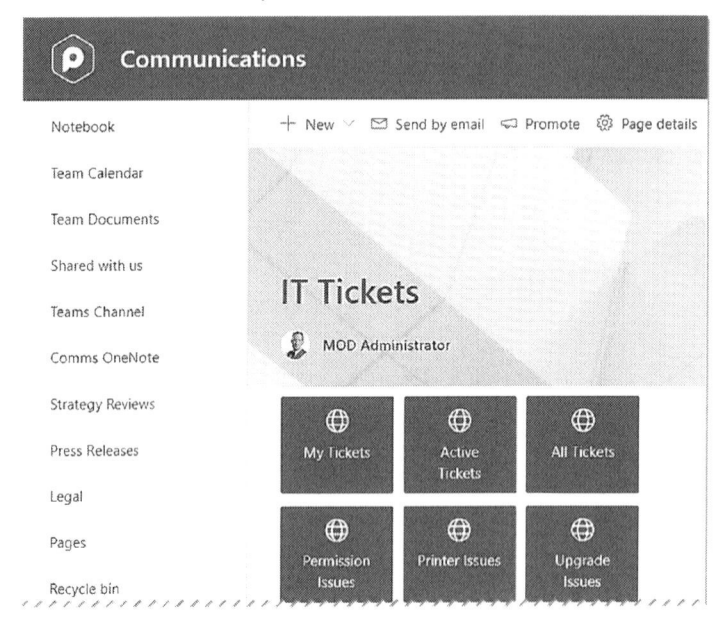

8.3.3 The Highlighted Content Web Part

In the Highlighted content web part, there is a possibility to show only links.

8.3.4 The Sites Web Part

In the Sites web part, links are shown as tiles on the page. This web part can only show links to sites within the tenant.

8.4 ADD IMAGES TO PAGES

Images make SharePoint pages more interesting, and sometimes an image can be more explanatory than text. The images can be fetched to the page from multiple sources, but you should consider how to do with updates.

When you add an image that you have no control over, for example from an external website, it will no longer be shown on your SharePoint page when it is removed from the original site. If the image is updated on the original site, it will be updated on your site too.

To have full control over the image, download it and add it to the page from your computer. Then it will be saved to SharePoint, and you don't risk losing it on the page. But this of course means that your picture will not be updated when the original picture is updated!

Be careful to only use creative commons or images that are free to share and use, when you take images from a website that you don't control. You can filter by license in the web browser.

8.4.1 Picture Options for Pages

The Hero and Highlighted content web parts can have both images and other content, but Microsoft also offers two modern web parts that are solely intended for images: Image and Image gallery. When images are added to one of these web parts, users can see the images, but they cannot do anything with them.

If you want to give users a possibility to work with the images, you can instead use the Document library web part.

8.4.1.1 Image Web Part

The Image web part is intended for one picture. When you add the web part to a page, the right pane will open so that you can select the image source.

Another option is to just drag an image to a page that is open in edit mode. The image will automatically be added to an Image web part.

When you have added the image, a toolbox will be displayed above it so that you can work with the image. From left to right, you can:

- Resize the image by dragging in the handles that appear when you click on the icon.
- Crop the image.
- Crop with aspect ratios.
- Align the image.
- Reset the image to the state it was when you last saved it.

- Save the change to the image.

When you click on the edit icon to the left of the web part, you can add a text overlay to the image. You can also add a link and an alternative text.

8.4.1.2 Image Gallery Web Part

If you want to add multiple images in the same web part, you can use the Image gallery web part. Here you can display selected images or show images dynamically from a document library.

In the Image gallery web part, you cannot resize or crop images, but you can choose between Brick, Carousel and Grid layout. The Carousel layout shows the images in a slideshow.

There are two ways to add images to an Image gallery web part:

- Click on the 'Add' button in the web part to open the right pane with the source options.
- Drag the images to the web part. In this case, you need to add the web part first. If you just drag multiple images to a page without an Image gallery web part, they will be placed in one Image web part each.

I suggest that you first add the images to the web part and then try different layouts with them. Generally, the Image gallery works best if the images are of similar size.

When you have added images to the Image gallery web part, click on the edit icon on each image to add text. Links are currently not possible here.

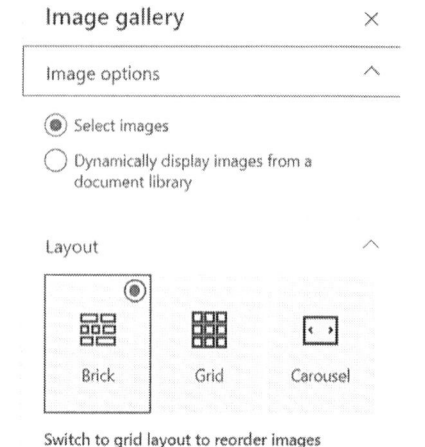

140

8.4.1.3 Document Library Web Part

Images can be added to a document library, or you can use the specific picture library that is designed for images. Such a picture library can be created from the "Your Apps" page.

When you add a Document library web part to a page, both document libraries and picture libraries can be selected in the web part.

Picture Library

Document library

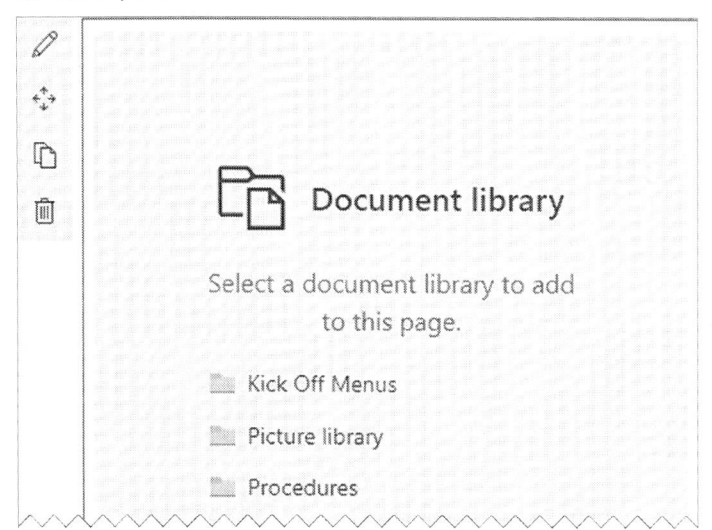

Select a document library to add to this page.

- Kick Off Menus
- Picture library
- Procedures

Adding images to a Document library web is a good option when you want to give users a possibility to work with the images, like downloading them and seeing their properties.

8.5 SUMMARY

In this chapter, you have learned how to create and customize modern site pages. I have also introduced the "Site Pages" library, where you can manage the settings for all pages in a site, and I have described how to schedule page publishing and set a page as homepage.

After some examples on web parts, I showed how images and links can be added to site pages.

Now it is high time to look at the SharePoint permissions. When you share content, it is important to consider the permissions you give, so I have included the sharing in the same chapter as the general permission information.

9 Permissions and Sharing

All SharePoint content is governed by permissions. If the permissions are set correctly, users will never see anything that they don't have access to, and they can never do anything they should not be allowed to do.

This means that you can feel sure that you have permission to use all links, buttons, items and so on that you see in your organization's SharePoint Online. It also means that you might not see all commands that are shown in images in this book.

9.1 Inheritance

SharePoint pages, apps, subsites and items, by default inherit the same permissions as the higher level. Apps inherit the site permissions, and pages and other items inherit the app permissions.

Therefore, users who have Edit permission on a site, by default also have Edit permission on all apps in that site, and they even have Edit permission on all items in each app.

9.2 SharePoint Groups

The permission levels in SharePoint are packages of connected permissions. Users who have the same permission on a site belong to the same permission group, also called SharePoint group.

Note that a SharePoint group is not the same as a Microsoft 365 group. In a Microsoft 365 group, colleagues share several resources and work together on them. In a SharePoint group, the only thing that is common for everyone is the permission level.

- Site Owners have Full control over the site content and can do anything with it – except perform actions that have been forbidden in the SharePoint or Microsoft Admin centers.

  By default, Site owners are also Site admins, but that can be changed in the SharePoint Admin center. If a separate Site admin has been appointed, the Site owner still has full control over all content in the site, but there are some limitations on what the owner can do in the site settings.

- Site Members have Edit permission, which means that they can view, add, update and delete apps, items and folders in a site.

- Site Visitors have Read permission. They can only view pages and items, but they can download files.

You can set site permission for people directly on a site or in an app, and when you do that, you normally use one of these pre-defined SharePoint groups.

When you create a site, SharePoint automatically creates a set of SharePoint groups for that site.

You can see the SharePoint groups and their members under the 365 Settings icon >Site permissions.

When you expand a SharePoint group, you can see all members of that group in Communication sites.

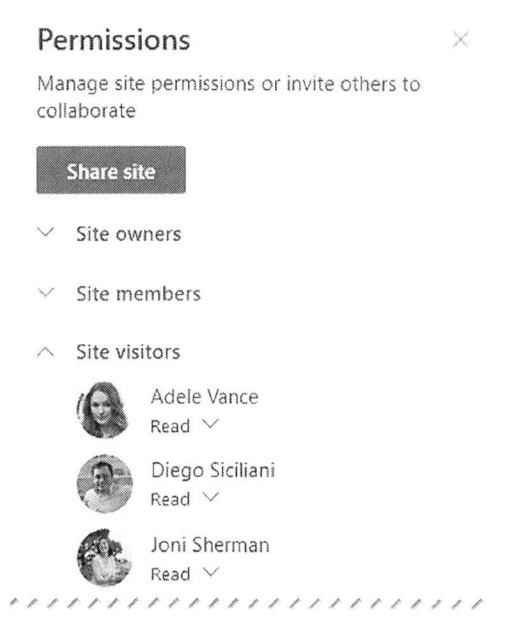

Permissions

Manage site permissions or invite others to collaborate

Share site

∨ Site owners

∨ Site members

∧ Site visitors

    Adele Vance
    Read ∨

    Diego Siciliani
    Read ∨

    Joni Sherman
    Read ∨

In Group Team sites, you will at first only see the SharePoint group, not the individual members. This way, you can change the permission level for the whole group.

∨ **Site owners**

∧ **Site members**

    OA Office 365 Adoption Members
          Edit ∨

∨ **Site visitors**

When you hover over the group, a dialog with member information will open.

9.3 SHARE A SITE

The settings for how much sharing should be allowed are made in the SharePoint Admin center for the whole tenant, and administrators can also limit sharing options for individual sites. Therefore, the options shown in the images below might be different in your organization.

Note that you share all the content of a site when you share the site.

9.3.1 Default Site Permissions

When you share a site, you can select Read, Edit or Full Control permission for each user or group that you share the site with.

The default permission level is different depending on site type:

- For Communication sites, the default permission option is Read.
- For Group Team sites, the default option is Edit. The default Home site also has Edit permission for all users.

As you see, the default permissions are extensive for Team sites, but site owners can restrict the options, and Global and SharePoint administrators can also restrict the options for the whole tenant. Site settings can never allow more than what is set in the tenant settings.

9.3.2 Share a Site with the Share Button

Communication sites have a 'Share' button in the top right corner. It opens a right pane, where you can add people and groups to share the site with and select their permission levels.

Start writing a name or e-mail address to get suggestions. Select one of the suggestions, and the person or group will be added below the field.

The default permission for the site type is assigned automatically, but you can change it before you share the site. This is done with the little arrow at the permission information below the name of the added person or group.

Continue in the same way to share the site with more people.

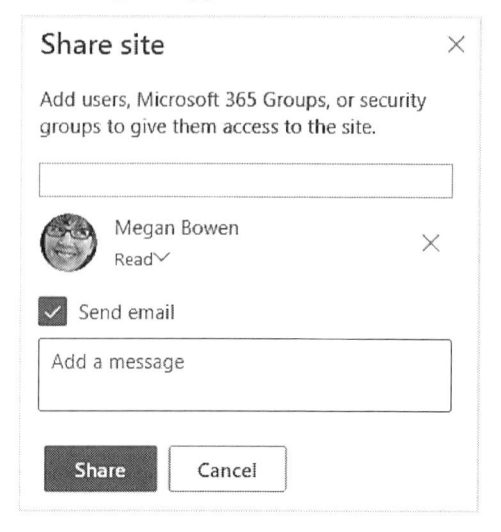

An e-mail invitation will be sent by default to the people you share the site with, and you can also add a message.

9.3.3 Share a Site from the Site Permissions Pane

The 'Site permissions' link under the 365 Settings icon opens a right pane where you can invite users and manage permissions and sharing settings. Here, you can share both Communication sites and Group Team sites.

9.3.3.1 Share from Communication Site

In Communication sites, the Permissions right pane has a 'Share site' button on top. When you click on the 'Share site' button, the same invitation pane opens as when you use the modern 'Share' button, *see* above.

9.3.3.2 Share from Group Team Site

Group Team sites have a button with the text 'Invite people' in the Permissions pane.

Permissions

Manage site permissions or invite others to collaborate

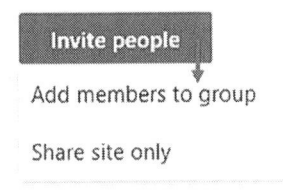

Invite people
- Add members to group
- Share site only

When you share a Group Team site, you can select to add the new people to the Microsoft 365 group or just to the site.

When you select to only share the site, the same right pane as with the 'Share' button will open.

If you select to add new members to the group, a new pane will open with an 'Add members' button. Here. you can see all the current members in the Microsoft 365 group.

The 'Add members' button opens the same right pane as the 'Share' button, see above.

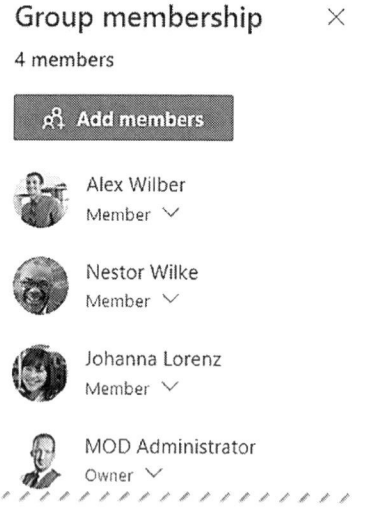

9.3.4 Share a Group Team Site with an External Guest

Site owners might be allowed to invite people outside the organization to a Group Team site. When external guest access is allowed, the guests are invited from Outlook, not from SharePoint.

1. Under Groups in Outlook, click on the group to which you want to invite guests.
2. Open the group contact card and click on the Members link.

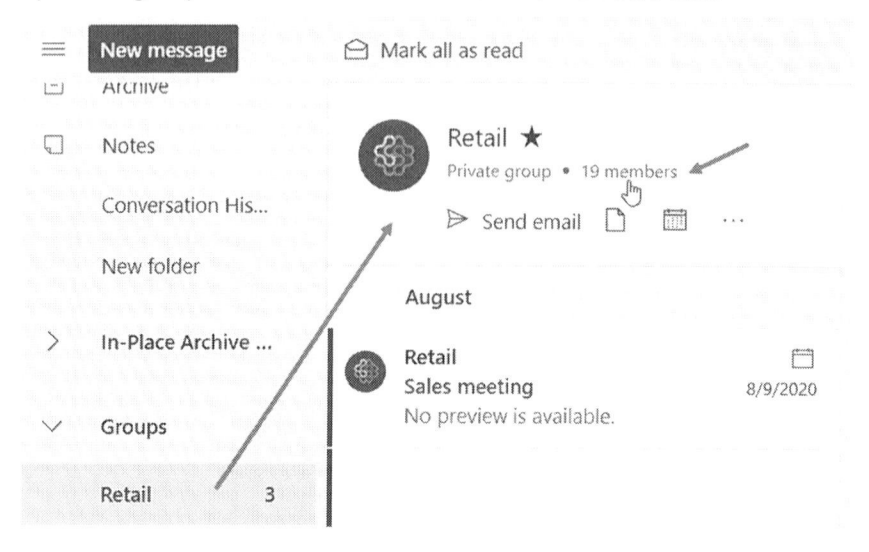

146

3. Click on 'Add members' in the dialog that opens.
4. Type the guest's e-mail address and then click on 'Add'.
5. Click on Close when you have finished adding guests.

9.3.5 Manage Site Members

Only Site owners can add and remove site members from sites and change SharePoint group for another group member. This is done differently in Communication sites and Group Team sites.

9.3.5.1 Manage Communication Site Members

Below the share button, the Permissions right pane in a Communication site shows the three SharePoint groups.

Here, Site owners can change member permissions and remove people from the site.

When you select another permission level, the person will automatically be moved to that SharePoint group.

If you, for example, change Allan Deyoung's permission (see the image to the right) from Edit to Full control, he will be moved to the Site owners SharePoint group.

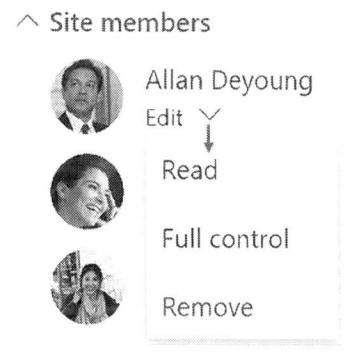

∧ Site members

Allan Deyoung
Edit ∨

Read

Full control

Remove

9.3.5.2 Manage Group Team Site Members

In Group Team sites, only the group name is displayed under the SharePoint groups in the Permissions pane. Here, the permissions for the whole SharePoint group can be edited but not the permission level for an individual member.

If you want to manage individual members, you can click on 'Invite people' in the Permissions pane and then select to add members to the Microsoft 365 group, as described in 9.3.3.2 Share from Group Team Site above.

Now all members are displayed, and you can change their status with the little arrow to the right of the current status.

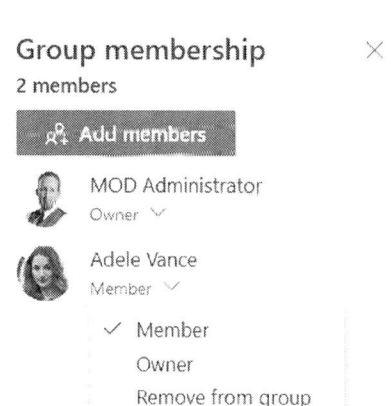

Group membership ✕

2 members

🧑 **Add members**

MOD Administrator
Owner ∨

Adele Vance
Member ∨

✓ Member
Owner
Remove from group

147

You can also manage the Microsoft 365 group in Outlook, in the same way as when you invite guests, *see* above.

1. Under Groups in the Outlook left menu, select the Microsoft 365 group you want to manage.
2. Click on the Members link in the group's contact card.
3. A dialog will open, where you can change permission level or remove users from the Microsoft 365 group – and thereby also from the site – with the x icon.

Adele Vance	Retail Manager	Member	×
Alex Wilber	Marketing Assistant	Owner Member ∨	×
Christie Cline	Buyer	Member ∨	×

9.3.6   Site Sharing Permissions

Site owners can click on the "Change how members can share" link in the 'Permissions' pane, to modify the sharing and access options. You can, for example, decide that only owners can share files, folders and the site.

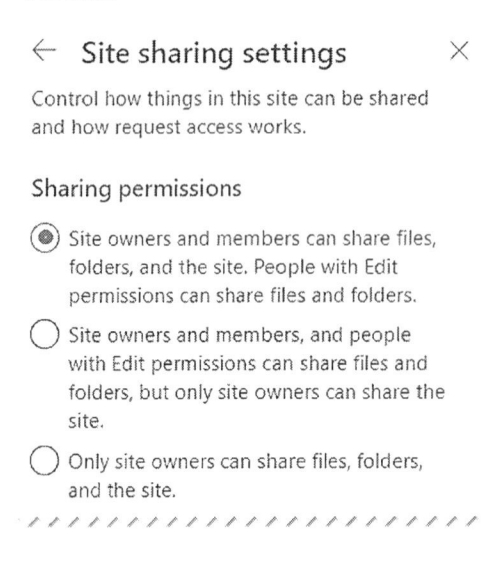

← **Site sharing settings**   ×

Control how things in this site can be shared and how request access works.

Sharing permissions

◉ Site owners and members can share files, folders, and the site. People with Edit permissions can share files and folders.

○ Site owners and members, and people with Edit permissions can share files and folders, but only site owners can share the site.

○ Only site owners can share files, folders, and the site.

9.3.6.1 Access Request

If someone who is not a site owner uses the 'Share' command to invite other people to a site, an access request for the site will be sent to site owners or to a specified e-mail address. If the invitation is accepted, the approver can specify the permission level for the user.

The access request also allows people to request access to content that they do not have permission to see.

When 'Allow access requests' is enabled, an e-mail with an access request will be sent to the specified e-mail address.

You can also reach the Access request settings from the Permissions right pane >Site sharing settings.

Access requests are enabled by default.

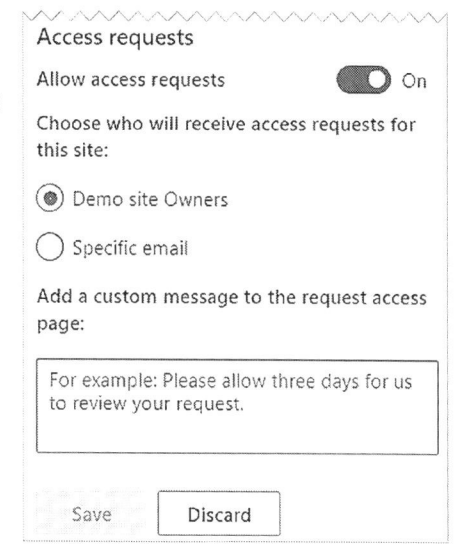

9.4 SHARE A FILE

Users with Edit permission can by default share files with people who don't have access to the document library where the files are stored. Here I will describe file sharing, because that is most common, but folders and list items can be shared in the same way.

Note that only the file will be shared even if you select the whole item when sharing from a document library. If you select a folder or a list item, all columns will be included.

When you share a file, the link in the e-mail will become a so-called short link, showing the document name and the file type icon.

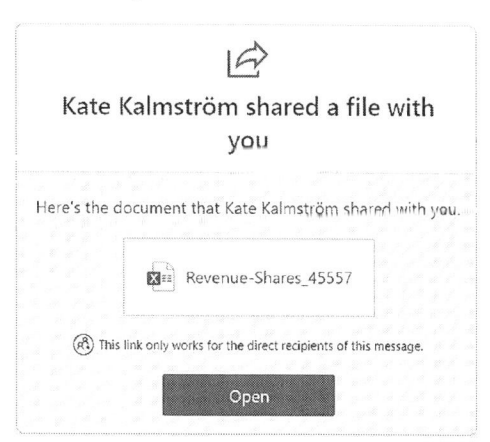

9.4.1 The 'Share' Command

To share a file select an item and click on the 'Share' button in the command bar. You can also click on the Share icon at the selected item or open the ellipsis and click on the 'Share' link.

A dialog opens, where you can give names or e-mail addresses to specific people or groups with whom you want to share the file. Above that field, there is a Permission selector.

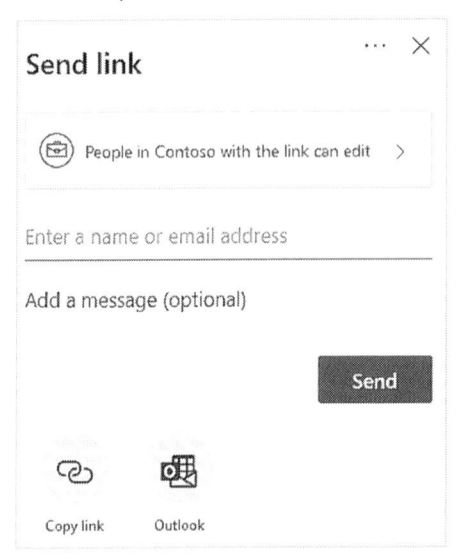

The Outlook option in the 'Share link' dialog, opens an e-mail with a link to the file.

You can – and should! – decide which people should be able to use the sharing link and if the link should give edit permission or not.

You must however click on the permission selector above the field where you fill out the person/group you want to share with, before you can see and change the permission you are giving. When you do that, a Link settings dialog will open.

The permission options are:
Anyone with the link, People in the organization with the link, People with existing access and Specific people. The number of options can be limited in the SharePoint Admin center, so 'Anyone with the link' might not be active.

I recommend that you think twice before you use the option 'Anyone with the link', even if it is available, because this option allows people outside the organization to access the file. They don't have to log in, so their access cannot be audited, and you cannot see who has used the file.

There are several other options to decide what people can do with the file:

- 'Open in review mode only' is only present when you share Word files. It lets a receiver without edit permission comment on the file but not edit it.

- When you uncheck the 'Allow editing' box, the 'Block download' option will be active, so that you can enable it if you want the recipient to be able to view the shared file but not download it.

    Currently, the download block works for Office files, PDF files, images, audio files and video files.

- If you have selected the 'Anyone with the link' option, you will get the option to set an expiration date and a password for the link. (If you set a password, you must distribute it yourself.)

    Click on the line at 'Set expiration date' to open a date and time picker – to click on the icon does not work!

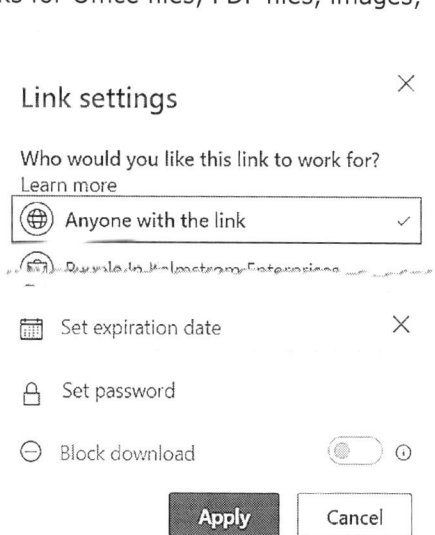

9.4.2 Share with a Link

Instead of sharing with the 'Share' command, you can send a link to the SharePoint content that you want to share. Only the people you have specified can use the link.

To have the correct link, use the command 'Copy link', which you can find in the command bar and under the item ellipsis.

Click on the people or group selection to see and be able to uncheck the 'Allow editing' box and block download, just as when you use the 'Share' command, see above.

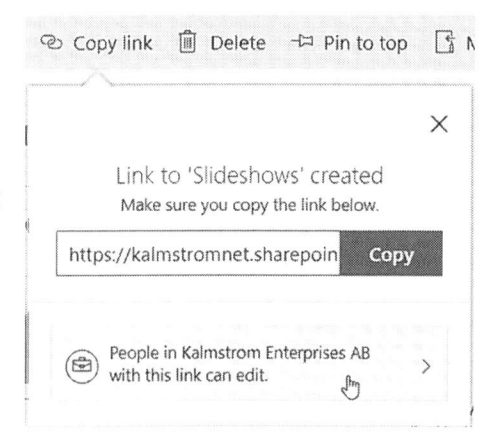

9.4.3 Manage Access

When you select an item, you can see in its Information pane with whom it has been shared. Click on 'Manage access' to have details on the sharing and permissions.

In the 'Manage Access' right pane that opens, you can easily edit the permissions from the dropdown at each user or group. Here, you can also stop sharing the file.

To grant access to more people, you can click on the icon with a plus above 'Manage access' in the Information pane. Now, you will have a simpler sharing dialog with just two permission options: Can edit and Can view. Use the 'Share' command to have more options, as described above.

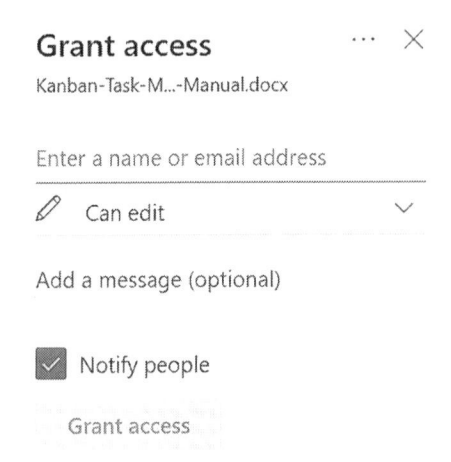

A link to the 'Manage access' pane is also available under the ellipsis at the item and from the ellipsis in the Sharing dialog.

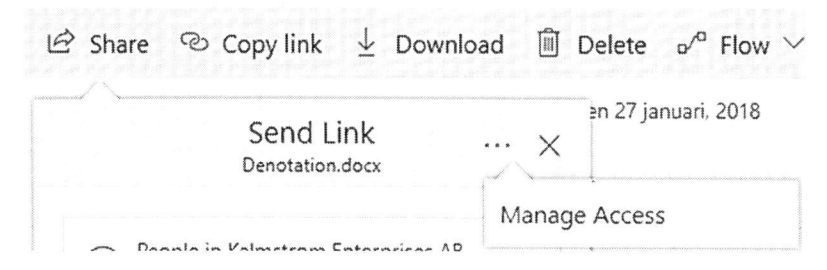

9.4.4 E-mail Attachments

When you click on the 'Attach' button in an e-mail that is open in Outlook on the web, you will have several options, and they give different possibilities to set permissions on the file:

- Browse the computer and upload a file.
- Browse libraries in OneDrive and SharePoint Online.
- Upload a file from the computer to OneDrive and share it from there.
- Attach a recently used OneDrive or SharePoint file.

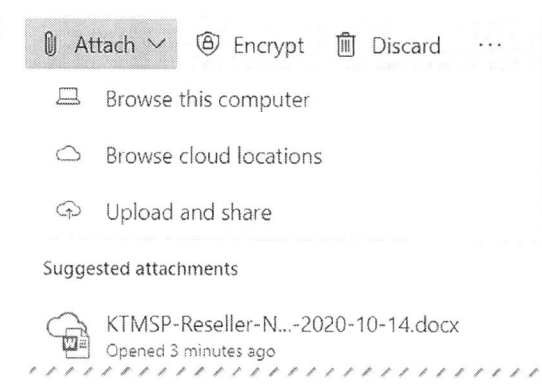

When you share an attachment from OneDrive or SharePoint, you are sharing a link to the file.

To share a link instead of the actual file saves mailbox space, and it also gives you a possibility to modify the permissions on the file. Another important benefit is that you are not creating a duplicate of the file. When users access the file, they will always see the latest version.

By default, the receiver will get edit permission on the file if it is an Office file, but in all options where the file is stored in the cloud, you will have a possibility to change the permission.

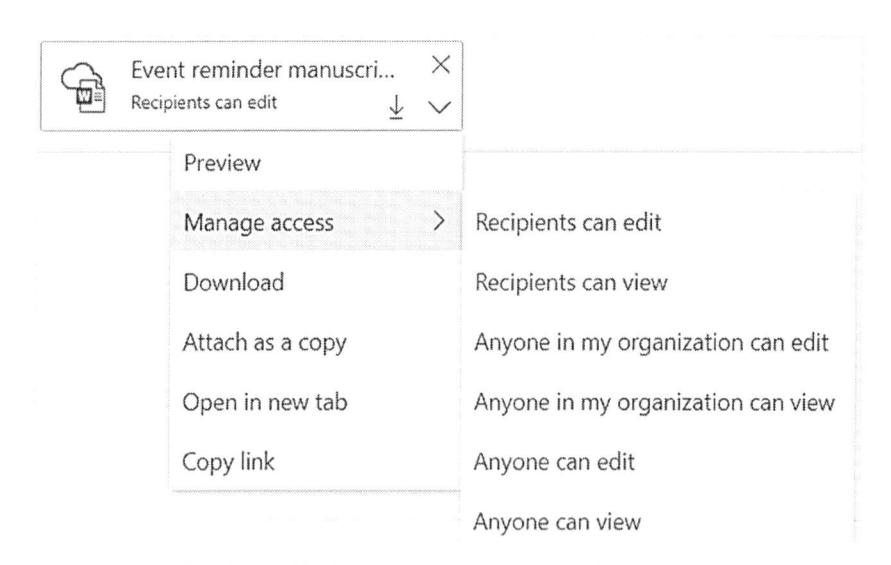

Preview	
Manage access >	Recipients can edit
Download	Recipients can view
Attach as a copy	Anyone in my organization can edit
Open in new tab	Anyone in my organization can view
Copy link	Anyone can edit
	Anyone can view

When you upload the file from your computer, there is no possibility to modify the permission. But when the file has been attached, you can upload it to OneDrive and then you will have the same options as in the image above. (It is of course quicker to use the 'Upload and share' option directly.)

Preview

Download

Upload to OneDrive - Kalmstrom Enterprises AB

Sometimes it is necessary to give the receiver(s) permission to edit the file, so that several people can edit the same copy of a file, *refer to* 5.6.2.1, Editing by Multiple Users. In other cases, it is more secure to limit the permission.

When users share Word files, the sharing e-mail will include information about the estimated time it will take a user to read the document as well as a list of the key points in the document. Files that have been marked as sensitive by Data Loss Prevention will not include that information.

9.5 SHARE A PAGE

SharePoint pages are files, so in the "Site Pages" library, pages can be shared in the same way as other files. Open the ellipsis at the page you want to share and click on 'Share'.

You will have similar permission options as when you share a file, but note that there is a checkbox for edit permission, and it is checked by default.

From the page, you can also share via the 'Promote' button in the command bar. The button opens a right pane with four options for sharing.

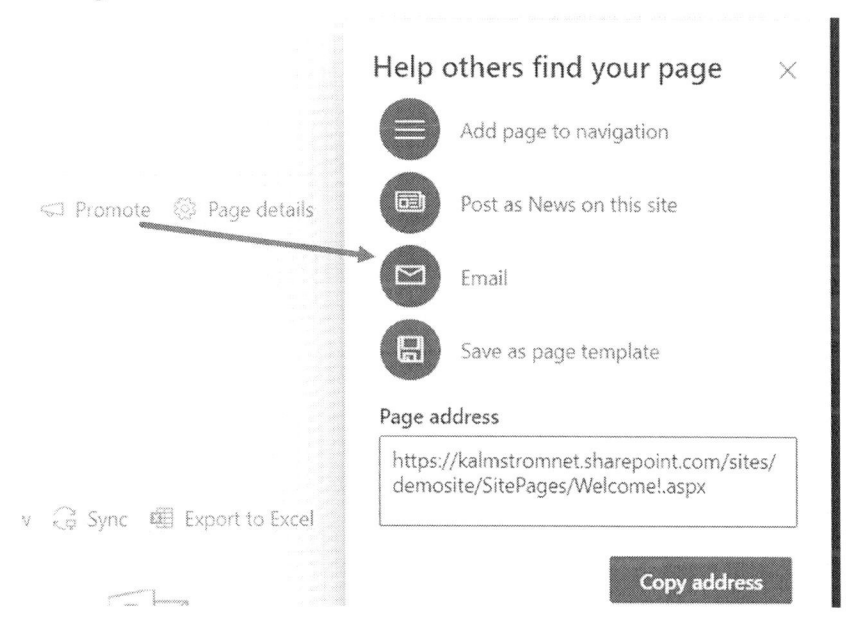

Help others find your page

- Add page to navigation
- Post as News on this site
- Email
- Save as page template

Page address

https://kalmstromnet.sharepoint.com/sites/demosite/SitePages/Welcome!.aspx

Copy address

When you click on 'Add page to navigation' and 'Post as News on this site', the action is taken immediately, and you don't need to do anything more.

The 'Email' link opens a dialog where you can enter an e-mail address and a message to send a link to the page.

When you save the page as a template, it will show up among the templates when users create another page on the same site.

9.6 STOP SHARING AN ITEM

To stop sharing a file, page or list item, open 'Manage Access' in the app where the item is stored. Click on 'Stop sharing' to remove all sharing.

[Screenshot showing a 'Manage Access' pane for Employee Sentiment Analysis.xlsx with options to Stop sharing, and entries for Alex Wilber (Marketing Assistant, Can edit) and Adele Vance (Retail Manager, Can view, Stop sharing).]

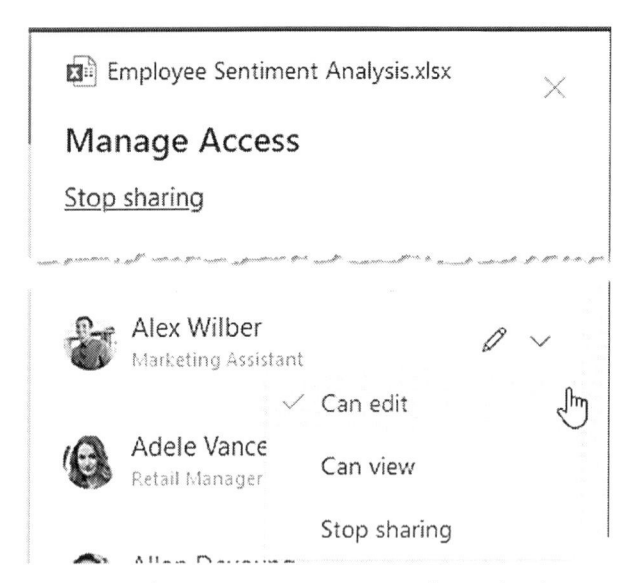

To stop only one person or group from sharing, open the dropdown for that person/group in the 'Manage Access' pane. (Here, you can also change the permission level for that person/group.)

9.7 Summary

SharePoint Online is a place in the cloud where teams and organizations can share content, but the sharing can get out of hand if you don't understand how the permission and sharing processes work.

In this chapter, we have looked at sharing via the 'Share' command, sharing by link and sharing to people outside the organization, and we have seen how you can restrict the default permissions when sharing.

You now understand how the SharePoint permission inheritance works, and you know the difference between Microsoft 365 groups and SharePoint groups.

In the two last chapters I will introduce two products that can be reached from and used with SharePoint: Power Automate and Excel Forms.

10 POWER AUTOMATE BUILT-IN FLOWS

SharePoint flows and workflows can be used in all kinds of SharePoint apps to automate time consuming processes. How to create flows and workflows is out of scope for this book, but in this chapter, we will look at the built-in flows that are available in SharePoint Online.

Microsoft Power Automate is a modern 365 automation service, and the workflows created with Power Automate are often called flows. Such flows can be used extensively for many cloud-based services, and several such services are often combined in one flow.

Power Automate has its own 'Automate' button in the command bar of the modern app interface. It gives some options to use built-in SharePoint flows that are very easy to create.

10.1 REMINDER

When an app has the modern interface and a custom Date and Time column, it gets a built-in flow to send an e-mail reminder any number of days in advance of a specific date.

You can enable the reminder flow under Automate >Set a reminder >the Date and Time column you want to use.

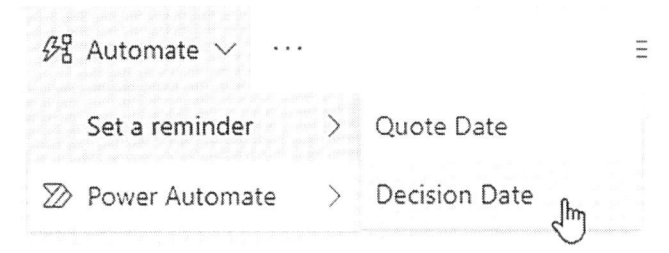

(If you cannot see the 'Set a reminder' option, the app does not have a *custom* Date and Time column. For example, the automatically created Date and Time columns in a calendar app are not custom columns and cannot be used in a reminder flow.)

A right pane with flow information will open. Here, you can sign in if needed, but in most cases, you are already signed in to the services used in the flow.

A green check means that you are signed in. A plus sign indicates that you need to sign in.

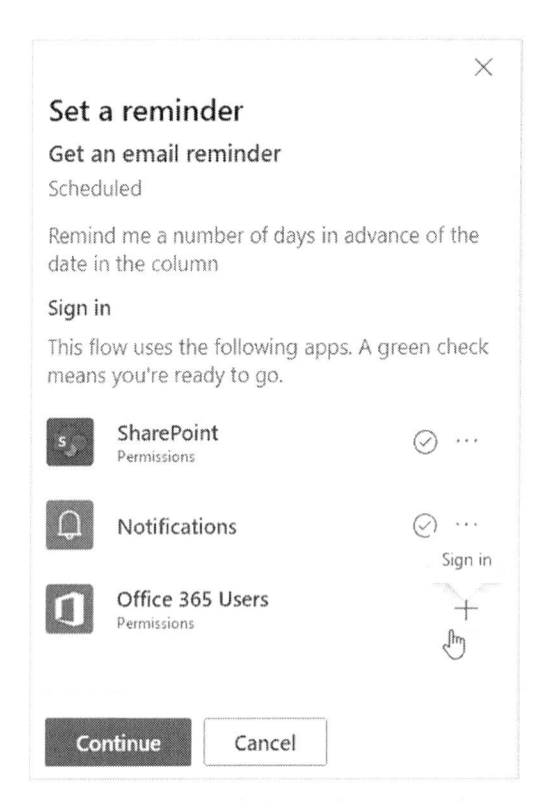

Set a reminder

Get an email reminder
Scheduled

Remind me a number of days in advance of the date in the column

Sign in

This flow uses the following apps. A green check means you're ready to go.

- SharePoint — Permissions ✓
- Notifications ✓
- Office 365 Users — Permissions

[Continue] [Cancel]

Click on 'Continue' when all services have green check marks.

When you have clicked on 'Continue', you can give the flow a name and decide how many days before the date in each item that you want to receive a reminder by e-mail.

To remove the flow, select 'See your flows'. You will now be directed to the Power Automate site, where you can click on the ellipsis at the flow and delete it.

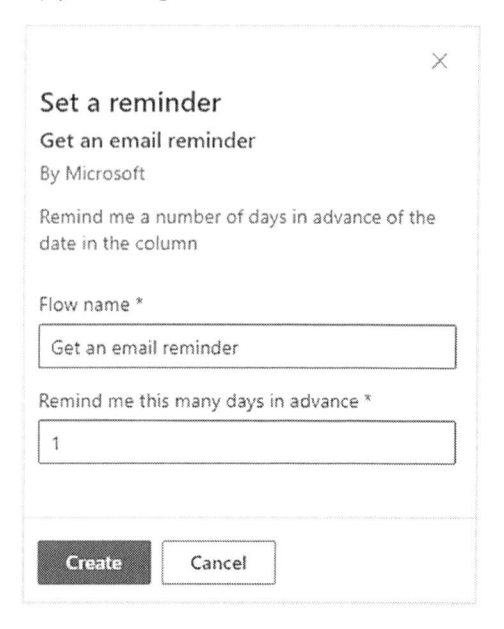

Set a reminder

Get an email reminder
By Microsoft

Remind me a number of days in advance of the date in the column

Flow name *

[Get an email reminder]

Remind me this many days in advance *

[1]

[Create] [Cancel]

10.2 REQUEST SIGN-OFF

All SharePoint apps that can have the modern interface, have built-in flows for requesting and giving approval on new app items. Here, I will describe the Request sign-off feature.

You can enable Request sign-off whenever you have created an app and want to give users a possibility to send documents or items to someone else for comments in an easy way.

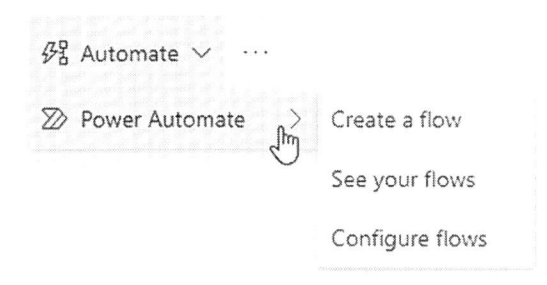

Click on Automate >Power Automate >Configure flows to open a right pane where you can set approvals on and off.

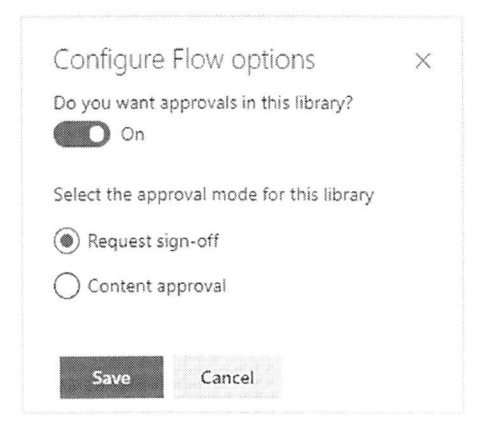

By default, the approvals feature is set to On, and the option Request sign-off is selected. You only need to click on 'Save' to enable the feature.

When approvals with request sign-off is enabled in an app, it is up to each author to ask for feedback on a new or updated list item or library file by running an approval flow. In libraries, it is the document that gets approved. In list apps, it is the whole item.

To run the sign-off flow, select the item, click on the 'Automate' button and select 'Request sign-off'.

A right pane will open, where you can see information about connectors and permissions, and connect if necessary, just as with the reminder flow. Then click on 'Create flow'.

Now, another right pane will open with fields for approver and a message. If more than one approver is added, anyone of them can approve the request.

When the flow is run, it sends an e-mail to the approver(s). When Microsoft Teams is used, there might also be a message under the Activity button.

All messages have a link to the file or item and buttons for approval and rejection, and there is also room for a comment that is sent to the requester.

The first time someone requests sign-off, a 'Sign-off status' column is added to the app. The value of the 'Sign-off status' column is blank for items where no request sign-off flow has been used.

The value is Pending when an item is sent for approval, and then either Approved or Rejected. The item can be seen by all users, whichever status it has.

To turn off the possibility to send Request Sign-off messages, select 'Configure flows' again and disable approvals.

10.3 APPROVE/REJECT PAGES

The "Site Pages" library has its own built-in approval flow. In many respects, the Page approval flow reminds of the Sign-off request flow. There are however important differences:

- The Page approval flow will apply to *all* pages in the library.
- The Page approval flow can be seen and edited on the Power Automate site >My flows.
- The new or modified page is hidden from other users than the approver and creator until it has been approved.

New and modified modern pages can be approved or rejected in the library, on the page, on the Power Automate site and in e-mails sent by the flow.

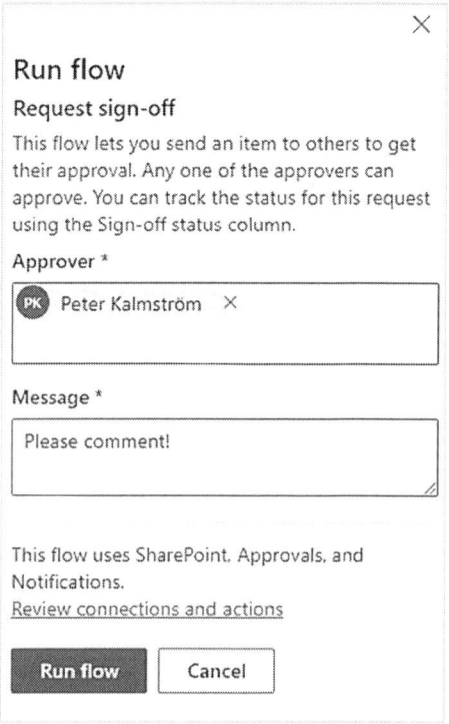

10.3.1 Configure the Flow

The modern "Site Pages" library interface has an 'Automate' button in the command bar, where site owners can configure the page approval flow.

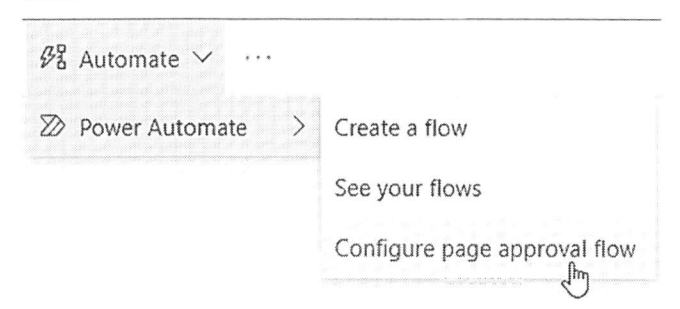

```
Automate ∨   ...
    Power Automate  >  Create a flow
                       See your flows
                       Configure page approval flow
```

When you click on 'Configure page approval flow', a right pane for the flow configuration will open. Click on 'Create flow'.

Configure page approval

Add a page approval flow to require approval before publishing new and updated pages in this library. Once approved, new and updated pages will be published.

Create flow

Learn more about page approvals

When you have clicked on "Create flow", you will have connectors information and a possibility to sign in, if needed.

When you click on 'Continue', you will be asked to give the flow a name and add approvers. These must have at least Edit permission over the site. By default, anyone of these approvers can approve.

When you click on 'Create', the approval flow will be created, and a new 'Approval Status' column will be added to the "Site Pages" library.

Create a page approval flow

Submit SharePoint page for approval

By Microsoft

When a new page is submitted for approval everyone on the approvers list will receive an email. Any one on the approvers list can approve the page. When approved, the page will be published for all readers and the approval status of the page will be Approved.

See less ∧

Flow name *

[Submit SharePoint page for approval]

Approvers *

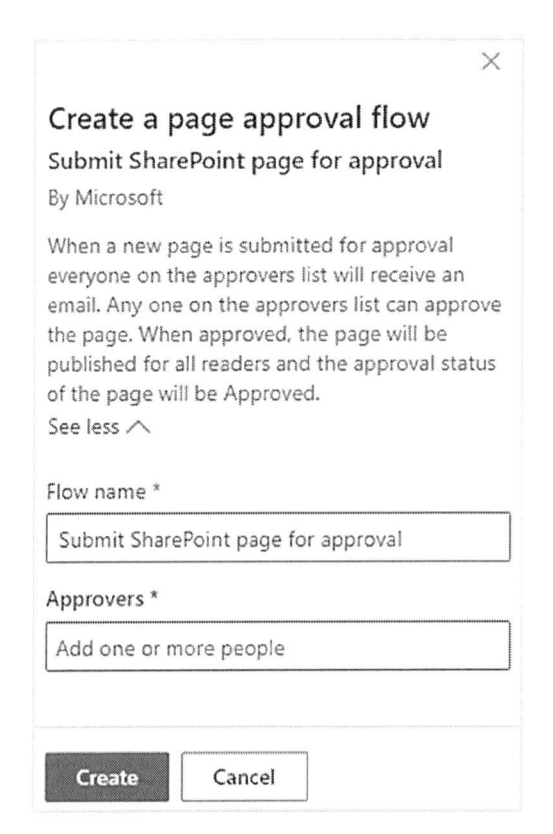

[Add one or more people]

[**Create**] [Cancel]

It is possible to add multiple flows, for different approvers. If another flow is created for the same "Site Pages" library, no additional status column will be added. All flows in the "Site Pages" library will use the same column.

When there is more than one flow, the person who submits the page for approval will have a selection in the upper left corner of the modern page.

Approval by Kate

Approval by Peter

10.3.2 Process

When page approval is enabled for the "Site pages" library, the 'Publish' button on the page is replaced by a 'Submit for approval' button, and the page author must enter a message in the right pane before submitting the page for approval.

✓ Your page has been saved   [📥 **Submit for approval**]

The page will be published automatically once it has been approved.

10.3.3 Turn Off Page Approval

In the "Site Pages" Library settings >Versioning settings, you can set the approval to No, to stop requesting approvals at page creation. You can also turn off or delete the page approval flow on the 'My Flows' page on the Power Automate site.

10.4 SUMMARY

In this chapter, we have seen how you can use the Automate button in the command bar to create flows that send reminder e-mails and e-mails for approval requests. These flows use the Microsoft 365 service Power Automate, a tool that can be used for much more than automatic e-mail sending.

With Power Automate, you can create custom flows that automate many kinds of business processes. How to create such flows for SharePoint is out of scope for this book, but I have described it the book *SharePoint Flows from Scratch*.

In the last chapter, I will introduce Forms, a survey service than can be reached from Group Team sites and OneDrive for Business.

11 THE FORMS SURVEY

SharePoint offers some different options when you want to create survey questions that colleagues can answer. Use a survey when you want to know people's opinion about things. You can also use a survey when you want to measure knowledge but not show the correct answers or give points for them.

In this chapter, we will have look at the Forms, an Excel service than can be reached from Group Team sites and OneDrive for Business.

Under the '+ New' command in Group Team sites Document libraries and in the default OneDrive for Business library, you can find a link to a simplified edition of the Microsoft 365 service Forms.

When you click on the 'Forms for Excel' link, the Forms site will open in a new tab.

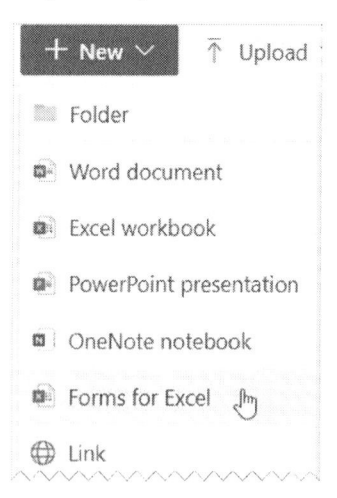

On the Forms site, you can add questions under the 'Questions' tab and see the answers under 'Responses' tab.

11.1 CREATE A FORM

When you click on the 'Add new' button on the Forms site, you will have several options on how people should answer your questions.

- For the 'Text' option, the answers must be typed in, but you can restrict them to be a number and even limit the number span.
- The 'Likert' option is easy to answer, because here the respondents just need to rate how much they think a statement is right or wrong.
- The 'Rating' option, just as the default 'Choice' and the 'Net Promoter Score' options, are also easy for respondents to fill out. They only need to select an option.
- When you select 'File upload', respondents can upload files to a new folder that will be created in SharePoint.
- With the 'Section' control, you can categorize the questions in a long survey, so that they will be easier for respondents to overview. Sections are especially useful when you want to branch the questions, *see* below.

When the first question has been finished, click on 'Add question' again to continue with the next one. The form is saved automatically.

11.1.1 Edit

Click on a question to edit it. In the top right corner of each question in edit mode, you can find icons for copying and deleting the question and for moving the question up and down in the form.

11.1.2 Branching

When the form is in edit mode, you can find an ellipsis in the bottom right corner of each question. One of the options is to add branching. (Some question types have more options under the ellipsis than subtitle and branching.)

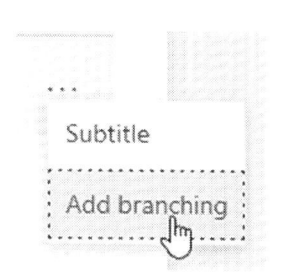

With branching, questions will have an option to continue in a specific way: to the next question, to another question or to the end of the form.

That way, you can follow up with questions that only apply to certain answers and/or let respondents skip questions that are not relevant to them.

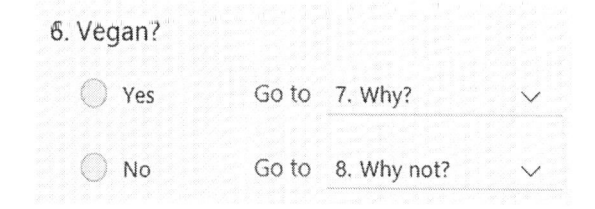

6. Vegan?

　　Yes　　　　Go to　7. Why?

　　No　　　　Go to　8. Why not?

11.2 SHARE THE FORM

Click on the 'Share' button in the right part of the command bar to share the form. Select one of the four options and copy the link/embed code if needed. These are the options:

- Copy a link and paste it in a shared area, for example a chat.
- Download a QR-code and paste it where your intended audience can scan it, for example with a mobile device.
- Copy the embed code and embed the form into a blog, a SharePoint page or other web page.
- Send a link in an e-mail by selecting the fourth option. This opens an e-mail with the link and some explaining, editable text. The first time you use this option, you must specify from what e-mail account the e-mail should be sent.

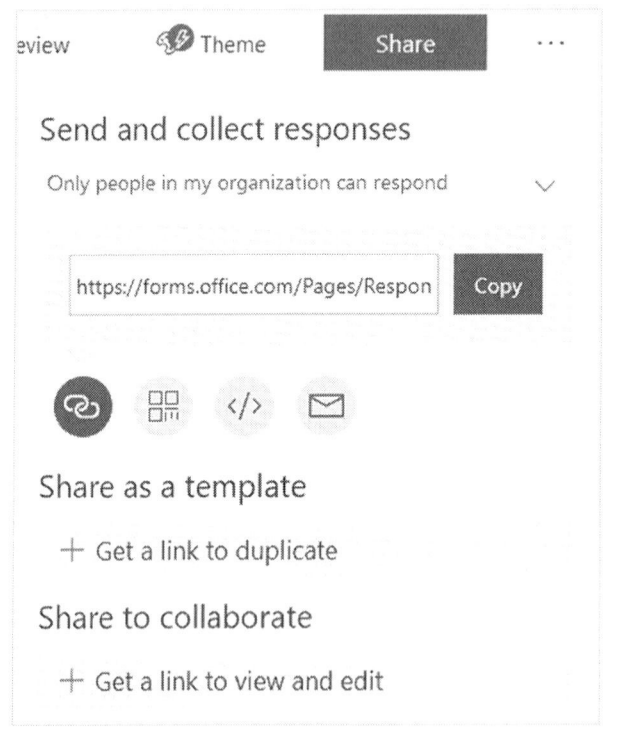

In the Share pane, you can also share the form to people who are not supposed to answer it:

- Get a template link. All receivers of this link can use the form as a template. Responses are not included.

- Get a collaboration link. Receivers of this link can work with the form, for example add or remove questions, see the responses and share the form with others.

By default, all users with a 365 work or school account can view and edit using this colloaboration link, but you can restrict the permission to people within the tenant or even specific people.

11.3 Check Form Results

To see the answers as they come in, open the 'Responses' tab on the Forms site and see statistics.

For more elaborate analysis you can open the results in Excel directly from the 'Responses' tab.

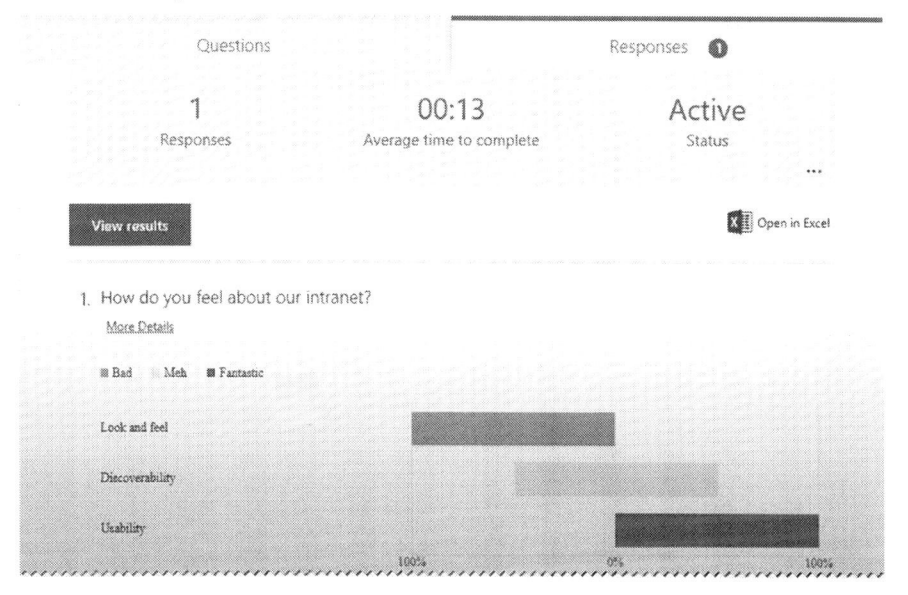

11.4 Form Settings

The Form settings are found under the ellipsis in the top right corner of the Form page. The image to the right shows the default settings.

The non-default options include a start and end date for the form and an e-mail notification of each response.

You can also set the questions to be shown in random order for each respondent (shuffle questions).

Settings

Who can fill out this form

◯ Anyone with the link can respond

◉ Only people in my organization can respond

☑ Record name

☐ One response per person

Options for responses

☑ Accept responses

☐ Start date

☐ End date

☐ Shuffle questions

☐ Customize thank you message

Notification

☐ Send email receipt to respondents

☐ Get email notification of each response

11.5 SUMMARY

The last chapter gave an overview of the Forms survey, a tool that you can use from all kinds of questionnaires.

I hope this book has given you a good understanding of what you can do with SharePoint Online and also a sense of security if you want to explore the possibilities further.

Thank you for reading my book!

About the Authors

Peter Kalmstrom is the CEO and Systems Designer of the Swedish family business Kalmstrom Enterprises AB, well known for the software brand *kalmstrom.com Business Solutions*. Peter has 19 Microsoft certifications, among them several for SharePoint, and he is a certified Microsoft Trainer.

Peter begun developing his kalmstrom.com products around the turn of the millennium, but for a period of five years he also worked as a Skype product manager. In 2010 he left Skype, and since then he has been focusing on developing standard and custom SharePoint solutions.

Peter has published eight more books, all available from Amazon:

- Excel 2016 from Scratch
- Microsoft Teams from Scratch
- Office 365 from Scratch
- PowerShell for SharePoint from Scratch
- SharePoint Flows from Scratch
- SharePoint Online Exercises
- SharePoint Online from Scratch
- SharePoint Workflows from Scratch

Peter divides his time between Sweden and Spain. He has three children, and apart from his keen interest in development and new technologies, he likes to sing and act. Peter is also a dedicated vegan and animal rights activist.

Kate Kalmström is Peter's mother and a former teacher, author of schoolbooks and translator. Nowadays she only works in the family business and assists Peter with his books.

INDEX

365 navigation bar, 11
365 settings icon, 15
365 theme, 15
Access requests, 149
Add a page, 120
add an app, 22
add column, 28
add content to web part, 127
Add shortcut to OneDrive, 72
add web part, 126, 127
Alert me, 48
Anyone with the link, 151
app display modes, 19
app filtering, 35
app interface, 22
App Launcher, 11
app layout, 41
app link, 25
app settings, 24
app template, 23
app types, 18
app web parts, 129
Append Changes to Existing Text, 65
associate with hub site, 97
associated site, 97
associated sites, 96
Attach button, 153
auto-created columns, 74
Automate, 157, 161
Blank list, 61
block download, 151
branching, 165
built-in approval flow, 159
built-in flows, 157
built-in reminder flow, 157
Button web part, 129
calendar app, 68
Calendar app, 68
calendar view, 43, 68
Call to action web part, 129
Change how members can share, 148
Change the look, 95
check out, 82, 117
Choice column, 31

collaborating on a document in Word Online, 82
column character limits, 29
column settings, 33
column type, 26
column types, 30
columns, 26
command bar, 22, 55
comments, 57
Communication site, 87, 89, 92
compare Word files, 53
conditional formatting, 38
Configure page approval flow, 161
copy files, 84
Copy link, 58, 81
Copy of this page', 121
Copy to, 73, 84, 119
create a file in a library, 79
create a form, 164
create a library, 74
create column, 26
Create Column page, 27
create list from Excel, 62
create list from existing list, 62
create list item, 58
create new view, 42
create page, 120
Create shared library, 113
Create site, 90
create view, 41, 43
data bar, 38
Date and Time column, 30
DateTimePicker, 30
default app view, 40
default file name, 80
default site permission, 144
default view, 41
delete app, 50
delete column, 49
delete item, 49
delete site, 101
delete view, 50
Delve, 16
disable page comments, 125
Divider web part, 129

document libraries, why?, 71
Document library web part, 129, 130, 141
document tile, 73
drag and drop files, 76
drag files to SharePoint, 76
Duplicate, 126
edit alert, 48
edit an Office file, 81
edit app form, 39
Edit Column page, 33
Edit columns, 39
Edit Event, 69
edit list items, 56
edit metadata, 34, 81
edit modern page, 123
edit multiple items, 34
edit page, 123
edit section, 126
edit survey question, 165
edit the New menu, 85
edit view, 41
edit web part, 126
e-mail attachments, 153
enhanced rich text, 64
Export to Excel, 56
external guest, 146
file editing by multiple users, 82
File Viewer web part, 128
Files On-Demand, 111
filter column values, 35
filter multiple columns, 36
follow site, 13
Form settings, 167
format column, 36
format view, 41
Forms, 164
Forms for Excel, 164
friendly date and time format, 30
Grid, 21
group items, 36
Group Team site, 87
Hero web part, 130
Highlighted content web part, 132, 138
Home site, 86
homepage, 86, 120
homepage templates, 89
hover card, 107
hub family, 96

hub permissions, 97
hub site, 96
Hub tab, 97
Image gallery web part, 140
Image web part, 128, 139
Information pane, 20
interface, 21
item, 18
Label, 99
library settings, 24
link expiration date, 151
link password, 151
links hierarchy, 101
Links web part, 137
list apps, 55
list settings, 24
list templates, 63
List web part, 129, 130
Location column, 32
make app view default, 41
make homepage, 120
Manage access, 152
manage site members, 147
mandatory check out, 83
manual sync, 109
metadata, 26
Microsoft 365 group, 88
Microsoft Lists, 59
Microsoft Teams, 89
modern list experience, 55
modern page, 121
modern picture options, 140
Move, 126
Move to, 73
Multiple lines of text, 64
My files, 103
My profile, 16
name a file, 80
navigation, 98
navigation hierarchy, 101
New Document, 79
new event, 69
News link, 136
News post, 135
News web part, 135
Office Online editions, 81
OneDrive for Business, 103
OneDrive settings, 104
OneDrive synchronization, 108

Open in review mode only, 151
page approval flow, 160
page comments, 124
Page details, 117, 133
page edit mode, 123
page sections, 125
page templates, 121
permission inheritance, 142
permission levels, 142
Permissions pane, 147
personal view, 40
Pin a thumbnail, 72
Power Automate, 157
profile picture, 16
promote page, 134
Properties, 73, 81
public view, 40
quick actions pane, 22
Quick Launch, 10
Quick Links web part, 137
recycle bin, 50
regional settings, 15
Rename, 73
rename a column, 39
rename a file, 78
renaming the 'Title' column, 75
request sign-off, 159
restore content, 50
restore earlier versions, 51
restore files, 53
restore OneDrive, 105
rich text, 64
save file to SharePoint, 77
save for later, 13
save page as a template, 122
scheduled publishing, 119
scheduling, 118
search, 14
second-stage recycle bin, 51
see form answers, 167
see version history, 52
select an item, 19
selective sync, 115
send link, 152
Share, 150
share a page, 155
Share button, 144
share file, 149
Share link, 150

share OneDrive files, 107
Share site button, 145
share survey, 166
shared resources, 88
SharePoint app, 18
SharePoint automation, 157
SharePoint groups, 142
SharePoint Online start page, 12
SharePoint sites, 86
Showcase, 90
sign-off, 159
Sign-off status, 160
Site, 128
Site admin, 142
site collection, 87
Site contents, 93
Site Member, 142
Site navigation, 10, 25
Site Owner, 142
Site Pages, 116
Site permissions, 143, 145
Site settings, 95
site types, 87
Site Visitor, 142
SitePages folder, 128
Sites web part, 138
sort column values, 35
Spacer web part, 132
Spaces, 136
Standard view display mode, 21
Standard view mode, 20
stop alert, 48
stop item sharing, 155
stop page approvals, 163
sub link, 101
subsite, 98
subsite, new, 98
Sync, 72, 108
sync issues, 111
sync settings, 111
Tasks and Issues alerts, 67
Tasks list, 66
team calendar, 68
Team sites, 87
Teams, 89
templates, 63, 84
timeline, 67
Title, 75
title area, 124

title field, 75
Topic, 90
Totals, 46
Upload, 72, 76
upload files, 76

URL, 36, 86, 116
version history, 51, 118, 133
View selector, 41
views, 40
Your Apps, 23, 70

Printed in Great Britain
by Amazon